AF570701

AWAKENED SOUL

Discoveries of healing, self-love and spiritual growth

Joanne Selinske PhD, Cht

AMARE PRESS

Awakened Soul: Discoveries of Healing, Self-Love and Spiritual Growth

First paperback edition December 2021

Cover design: Robin Vuchnich
Copyeditor/Proofreader: Marni MacRae
Cover photo: Ethan Jollie

Library of Congress Control Number:2021935594

Cataloging-in-Publication Data on File with Publisher

ISBN (Hardcover) 978-1-7368218-0-0
ISBN (Paperback) 978-1-7368218-1-7
ISBN (eBook) 978-1-7368218-3-1

Published by: Amare Press
Baltimore, Maryland

Visit the author's website at
www.JoanneSelinske.com

*. . . to the Source of all love,
and to all those whose love has graced
my life.*

PREFACE

We all want to live a happy wonderful life but, sadly, too few people actually do so. We struggle with how hard life can be while hardly having a clue about what life is for, nor what we can do with it. Imagine if you could understand the deep purpose of human life and clearly see how to get the ideal life that you most desire. In this book, Dr. Joanne Selinske gives you the knowledge to make your dreams come true.

Many books have been written about 'secret' laws that govern our lives but, in fact, those laws are not hidden from us. Rather, they are written large across the universe for all to see if you can look that large. It is like the Nazca Lines in Peru where you can't see the picture from the ground but have to be high up in the sky. When you discover your own past lives and the experiences you have had in between lives in the interlife, you remember who you really are and what you are here to do with your life. Dr. Selinske is an expert hypnotherapist with much experience regressing people back to past lives and the interlife in order to show you the big picture.

And the big picture is fascinating. ***Awakened Soul*** clearly shows the specific challenges that your Soul moves you through in developing you from a human animal to a divine human being. The case examples are so concrete and gripping that you will clearly see that you are already actively progressing in your soul's journey. Expect to feel renewed excitement about the life you are living and how to make it even better. Plus, you will get a taste of divine bliss, your very nature.

—DR. RICK LEVY, Author
Miraculous Health: How to Heal Your Body by Unleashing the Hidden Power of Your Mind;
The Happiness Sutra: How to Live a Heroic Life, Free of Stress

Introduction

This book is about your soul's destiny to awaken to the fullness of love and the joy and peace that are your companions.

Your higher self and spirit guides have led you to this book. It is not accidental. Happiness, love, and harmony are what they wish for you. They have been encouraging you to gather clues to the mosaic that is your eternal nature and life, the Akash, as it is known to many. Traces abound. They await discovery in dreams, spontaneous recall, books, seminars, spiritual regression sessions, and within the pages that follow. They are the individual pieces to your eternal montage.

Eons ago, your soul individuated from the Creator Source and set out on a journey through time; a journey called life. Initially, it was preoccupied with the challenges of physical survival and then moved on to mastery and success in the exterior world. Over time, it sensed that something was missing and the longing for it stirred. It sought fulfillment through its connection to others. But too often, this outward search ended in disappointment, pain, and even despair.

As your soul matured, it began to focus more on its interior world. Eventually, your soul remembered with greater ease that it is part of the divine essence that exudes joy and peace; the essence that is absolute love. As you journeyed on, even the faintest recall of this bliss drove it to crave more.

All along the way, your soul has been guided by an invisible, internal compass that is leading it back to the Creator Source to awaken.

Despite knowing that the curriculum was arduous, your soul enrolled in the Earth school to achieve a purpose. In each of its countless lives, it had a plan that it hoped to accomplish. Through these plans, your soul sought to learn, heal, balance, and serve.

Along the way, it had many adventures and countless discoveries. Some of them brought satisfaction and happiness, while others brought sadness and pain. Through it all, you grew stronger and wiser.

Once you get used to the idea that you incarnate countless times, it is easier if you learn to put your current struggles into the context from which they arise. Life can be entertaining and satisfying, as well as gripping and torturous.

On the way to awaken to this happiness, your path may have become littered with false beliefs about value and worth. Low self-esteem and self-acceptance, doubt, an inability to overcome loss or forgive, and failure to care for and love oneself are among the common scars. All preclude calm and rob you of stillness and inner peace. These problems present as everyday challenges for millions, including those who are consciously working on their spiritual growth. Overcoming these obstacles is essential to eliminate physical, emotional, and spiritual dis-ease and to promote physical, emotional, and spiritual health. ***Awakened Soul*** demonstrates the healing power of uncovering and replacing distorted beliefs and unhealthy self-talk.

I came to write this book after realizing that despite their diversity, my clients shared something significant in common. They were, on the whole, seekers of the truth of our eternal nature and experiences. Many were in the process of reconciling what they viewed as the limitations of their religious upbringing. Most were actively pursuing spiritual growth. What they also shared was the struggle to deepen their capacity for love. In their stories, you may identify with the struggles to overcome the barriers to love—to loving others and to love yourself.

Too often, thoughts about love are relegated to our experience of love within relationships. As communal beings, we experience life through our interactions with others in the outer world. Obviously, this is true, but ultimately, awakening requires work in the interior world to release false beliefs and limiting emotions. Past experiences shape our beliefs about love and thread through our emotional experiences.

Whether your experience of love has been challenged by loss or whether it has become mired in the quicksand of human interactions, you can be certain that, eventually, you will master love. Our struggles deepen our capacity for love, so that we are finally able to connect deeply with the divine essence—to awaken to its full experience and expression. The journey is often cloaked in mystery. In truth, it is about trudging through the challenges of human life, overcoming trials and tribulations that have burdened through myriad incarnations, and finally finding the peace and joy that rests within.

A hypnotherapist and spiritual counselor, I am very fortunate to have the second-hand benefit of my clients' forays into the realm of timelessness. My role as escort and facilitator affords regular opportunity for me to journey to the realm of love and unity. As a fellow traveler on the spiritual path, I am at once mindful of the benefit of achieving inner peace while constantly aware of how out of reach it might seem at any moment in time.

Not long ago, I facilitated a regression for a client. We set out with the intention of uncovering the past life correlates of his current sense of unease. For decades, he'd struggled to be accepted and loved. Both were conditional on being a good child, one who never veered from his family's strict code of ethics and behavior. He became a dutiful son and later a dutiful family man, all the while yearning to be loved for who he is and not what he could do for anyone.

He gleaned many details about the circumstances of earlier lives that fixed this pattern, uncovering the illusion at the heart of his current discontent. Past life circumstances had taught him that love and acceptance could only be found externally. He realized that what he pursued so vigorously was quietly and patiently waiting within. As he connected to his divine essence, he experienced pure love and unconditional acceptance. He found the roadmap to the joy and equanimity that he hopes will pervade the rest of his life.

Awakened Soul shares the journey of transformational healing of other clients who struggled to deepen their capacity for love. Told through transcripts of their spiritual regressions, the book focuses on problems common to those seeking emotional relief. The chapters that follow include the experiences of those I have guided on past life, life between lives, and other transpersonal hypnotic journeys. My selection of cases for inclusion in this book was very purposeful. No stranger to the journey, I recognized in each of their stories the wisdom they contained. In shared triumph, the featured clients teach us how uncovering distorted beliefs enabled them to overcome the impediments to self-love and deepen their capacity for love.

Each opted for a hypnotic regression experience to expand their understanding of love, to deepen their capacity to love others, and ultimately fully love themselves. For many of those you meet in the following chapters, the lessons of love were packaged in pain and loss. For all, the insights and healing they received have offered a road map to peace and joy in this life.

Throughout this book you will see references to the several different types of spiritual regression—past life, life between lives, and transpersonal journeys. Differences aside, each session is facilitated by a hypnotherapist, but what transpires is orchestrated by your higher self and your spirit guides.

In a past life regression, people journey to one or more past lives that have been catalogued in their Akashic Records. You journey to an earlier incarnation to explore events, circumstances, and relationships that shaped your beliefs. It is these core beliefs that souls carry forward into future lives and help you to understand current emotions, expectations, and beliefs. Recalling past lives enables you to view the experiences of the past, consider them from the perspective of the higher self, and understand the relationship of the past to current patterns of thinking, behavior, and relationships. Movement does not always follow linear time, especially when the person is reexperiencing lifetimes spanning different historical periods.

Life between lives ® (LBL) is a technique developed by Dr. Michael Newton for journeying to the spirit world—often referred to as the afterlife or interlife. In this unfiltered soul state, a wide range of experience awaits. These include meeting with soul family members, spirit guides, and advanced spiritual advisors; exploring interlife occupations, training, and hobbies; and discovering your soul's plan. As you access soul-based memories, you gain insight about your current and past lives through the soul's eternal perspective. A life between lives session is aptly described as peering into the window of your soul's eternal journey.

Transpersonal journeys are forays into the nonphysical realm of consciousness and connect you to your eternal awareness. They allow you to experience that vaster dimension of self, to engage with guides and other advanced spiritual beings, as well as to connect to members of our soul family. Less structured than either past life or life between lives sessions, they afford opportunities to focus on your most significant issue. By the broadest of definitions, past life regression and life between lives hypnotherapy are all transpersonal experiences.

Each of these hypnosis sessions begins with relaxation and visualization that enable the body to still and the mind to quiet, enabling focused concentration. Once in this deeply relaxed state, you can more readily connect to your higher self. There is a commonality of experience, while at the same time; each person's session reflects their unique soul nature and experience. Reconnection to the soul state brings peace, joy, and experience of absolute and unconditional love.

The themes covered in this book are universal. You likely will see parallels in your own life, even if the details of the clients' lives differ from your own. The case stories in this book are layered with wisdom. You may find that meandering through the chapters provides the best way to fully absorb it. I encourage you to apply what resonates.

Some believe that a regression experience alone can instantly heal. Most who choose the experience accept that work remains. For many, the healing they experience becomes the fuel for the work that follows. They realize that the insights gleaned offer directionality to reshape beliefs and coping behaviors. This is the work that must follow to achieve equanimity.

Most, if not all of us, have suffered in our many lifetimes. In his teachings, the Buddha spoke of necessary suffering, that is the suffering that is endemic to life and can't be avoided. He also spoke of unnecessary suffering, that is a result of our thoughts, hopes, and expectations. While we can't control the first, for example debilitating sickness or the death of a loved one, we can mitigate the second by changing our viewpoint about the suffering.

It takes courage and the strength to be vulnerable and to share one's story. And while they remain anonymous, the contributors hope that by sharing their experiences, you will overcome dis-*ease* and find the happiness and peace that you deserve. The transcripts are excerpts from their sessions and have been edited for clarity. I am deeply grateful to each of them for agreeing to share the details of their journey to awaken to love.

I hope that you will glean an understanding of how to eliminate unnecessary suffering from the wisdom and healing that each found. I know that your soul desires to find a more direct path to the peace and joy that awaits. Connecting to our divine essence is the collective destiny for all souls. One that I trust will be hastened by your own efforts to awaken.

CONTENTS

We are not human beings having a spiritual experience.
We are spiritual beings having a human experience.

—PIERRE TEILHARD DE CHARDIN

1

You Are A Spiritual Being Having A Human Experience

Teilhard de Chardin's words are not only a stirring reminder of your eternal nature, but they hint of the grand context within which human life unfolds.

You are a spark of divinity, not only made in the image and likeness of God, but in fact made of the same substance as the Creator Source. You are an eternal being who was birthed at a moment in time to experience life from a singular perspective. From the time of your individuation, you have circulated through a series of lifetimes in the physical and astral realms in a process known as reincarnation. From that moment on, you have been on a long but certain journey to awaken to your divine essence.

This is your soul's destiny and deepening your capacity for love is how it is realized.

The idea of eternal existence in heavenly realms can be found in the Abrahamic traditions, Hindu, Buddhist, and Eastern religions. Overlooking nomenclature and stratification differences, life after earthly death is a foundational belief of all of the great religious traditions.

Understanding your eternal nature provides the context for the challenges you encounter and offers direction to end your pain and suffering.

The soul's journey through eternity is anything but haphazard. Case study research of the thousands who have experienced spiritual regression paint a clear picture and resonate with the hundreds whose regressions I have facilitated. As you will read in the stories that follow, souls are planful about upcoming lifetimes. Each lifetime affords rich opportunity to overcome the obstacles keeping you from awakening, the mission that is at the core of your many forays into earthly life. Ever expanding and growing, your soul incarnates countless times before it has grown sufficiently to revel in the absolute love of the Creator Source.

In the time between lifetimes, you assess your progress, which gives purpose and direction to future incarnations. Readying for an upcoming incarnation, your soul makes a plan for what it hopes to accomplish. These plans reflect your soul's character and involve members of your soul family. Deepening your capacity for love is the motivating force.

Soul Plans

Eternity provides the soul endless opportunities for growth: to learn, to heal, to balance, to serve, and, ultimately, to awaken to its divine essence. These are the categorical purposes of plans made by souls for upcoming lifetimes.

The soul planning process includes decisions about readiness, difficulty, and the specific objectives to include in the life plan. The thread connecting the many life plans is the soul's quest to deepen its capacity for love and to awaken fully to its divine essence. Over your lifetime, your higher self and spirit guides constantly guide you as you execute your plan. Initially, their guidance is subtle. But if ignored, and you veer off plan, their messages grow less gentle. Occasionally, getting through the personality's outer shell requires stronger measures. A disconnect between your soul's preferences and your life choices can cause physical, emotional, and spiritual suffering.

In the interlife, between incarnations, you consolidate your lessons. The wisdom you acquire influences selection of circumstances and events for your next lifetime. Those that will fuel growth weigh heavily in the selection. Souls have different interests, and these interests are reflected in the life plans they craft. Those interested in justice will embed lessons about justice and injustice in life plans, while those interested in power will select life roles that enable power-powerlessness to play out. Not all life themes require mastery by all, although certain themes do. These include love, compassion, acceptance, and surrender. Through its many lifetimes, the soul needs to come to a full and balanced understanding of each of these. Said simply, it must learn all the lessons embedded in both mandatory and elective courses of Earth-school.

If the Earth-school analogy works for you, consider this; newer souls starting at the elementary level set out to master survival in the physical world. Tribal communities afford early experiences to survive. Souls progress to a middle level where they seek success; success as human beings, family members, friends, colleagues, citizens, and collaborators, as well as success in avocations and occupations. At this level, success is manifested in the exterior world. Finally, souls enter the analogous secondary level and take on the lessons of love—love of others and ultimately love of self. There is some fluidity within the three levels of soul growth, enabling return to earlier lessons and achievement.

As I prepare individuals for upcoming spiritual hypnosis, they are often surprised to hear beforehand that they may discover that they have already lived hundreds of lifetimes. There is no fixed number of lives that must be experienced. This is ultimately determined by the pace of mastery. Free will exerted throughout many lives may hasten one soul's progression, while slowing another's.

The higher self knows what is best for you. Understanding this, and that everything significant that happens to you, positive or negative, was planned by your soul, is comforting. Accepting and surrendering to it, is yet something else.

Character of Souls

As the soul moves through lifetimes, it manifests a character of its own. A soul is as unique as the human personality it embodies. And much like human personalities, the soul's character is multi-faceted. Each has different interests, ideas, acuities, preferences, temperaments, strengths, weaknesses, and a reservoir of experiences. These character differences are reflected in the choices embedded in soul plans and how the plans are realized during an incarnation.

For example, a soul who is temperamentally ambitious and wants to accomplish complex lessons quickly may overload a life plan, and in so doing create additional lessons and healing that will require future resolution. A soul that is very gregarious and enjoys support through its many relationships may get confused because it is trying to incorporate the advice that it has gotten from too many other people. The resulting confusion precludes clarity and may delay learning the lessons that were incorporated in the life plan.

At any point in time, you are the sum total of your physiology, soul's character, and all of the experiences you have had in the physical world and the astral heavens.

Soul Family

Clients relay from their regressions that we are not alone on our earthly journeys. Souls are traveling through eternity with a group of other souls—a soul family. Soul families vary in size. The largest I have encountered includes 246 different souls. Members of a soul family assume different roles over the course of lifetimes. A soul that agrees to assume a parental role in one lifetime may have been a spouse in one or more previous lifetimes. Simply said; different lifetime, different role.

The degree of spiritual connection varies among soul family members. Just like with large families, some are close, like the members of a nuclear family, while others are similar to distant cousins. The most important roles are assumed by the souls who are more spiritually intimate.

Soul families are important because you spend much of your earthly lives embedded in relationships. Much of what people learn about life is in relationship with others. Stop and think about it. Sure, you can gain information by reading and collecting details. You can fill your mind with detail upon detail. But truly mastering something happens when the information is applied in your exterior experience, most often; in relationship to someone else.

Those who enjoy theatre may find the analogy of a repertory company helpful. Repertory theatre relies on a resident company of actors.

For the production of one play, actors are cast in one role. For subsequent productions, those same actors are cast in the roles specific to the new plays. The defining variable in who is selected to play each role is who is best able to act the part. This is the same for the soul who looks to his soul family to decide who is best suited to play each of the key roles in an upcoming life.

Occasionally, an actor with a different skill set is not available in the resident company and is recruited from elsewhere. Similarly, sometimes a soul may need to cast someone from a neighboring soul group to play a specific role in the upcoming life.

The nature of the play, like the nature of the upcoming life, shapes the roles that are assumed by the various actors. The roles assumed by soul family members are both positive and negative. The determining factor is how the assumed role will assist the person to accomplish the soul's unfolding life plan.

Decisions to play a role in someone's upcoming life are made totally out of the bond of love that the souls enjoy, regardless of whether the lifetime role will be positive or negative.

Awakening to Love

Awakening to love becomes the priority as the soul matures and easily incorporates the lessons of earlier phases, once it has overcome challenges, healed, and balanced distorted beliefs. That is not to say that there are no loose ends to tie up once the soul begins to focus on love, but once in this third phase, its preoccupation is love.

Imagine a wire mannequin mimicking a human shape with light brilliantly radiating from within. Now picture hundreds upon hundreds of dirty pieces of fabric being layered over it. Likely the radiance of the light is no longer visible. Now, one by one, see the dirty cloths removed until the radiance of the light beam shines brightly through again.

You are like a mannequin, and the dirty fabric is the residue that sticks to you after earthly incarnations. The thickening smut from life's trauma quickly overshadows the light. The false beliefs that have been shaped, painful emotions endured, and out-of-balance coping behaviors eventually obscuring the light all together. It is quite an achievement if you manage to complete a life without collecting more residue.

One of the principles impacting human life is that the beliefs you hold affect what you feel and how you behave, echoing back in turn to what you believe. Over the course of a single lifetime, there are myriad opportunities for false beliefs to form, which in turn cause emotional imbalance and misdirect ensuing behavior.

Your feelings are a signal of how aligned your choices are to your soul's intention for this lifetime. The following is illustrative. A person who has been betrayed may conclude that people are not trustworthy. This belief prompts the individual to fear forming relationships. Fearing the pain of betrayal, a person likely will avoid at least some relationships; and if the original betrayal was dramatic, the individual may isolate himself from everyone.

One of the universal principles guiding spiritual advancement is balance—balance of thoughts, feelings, and behaviors. Even this straightforward example hints at the onerous challenge the soul faces as it journeys through its many lifetimes.

To achieve requisite balance, the soul willingly incorporates imbalance left unresolved at the end of earlier lifetimes into a future life plan. A younger soul may incorporate a single matter, while a more experienced soul may embed multiple imbalances.

The soul understands, through its earthly experiences, that turmoil motivates. And so, as if it has forgotten its prior experience of pain, it willingly embeds challenges into its life plan. In setting up a paradoxical conundrum for itself to resolve in the upcoming life, it almost assures some degree of pain to achieve the desired goal. The intent is not to suffer but to resurrect the emotions and beliefs that were left unbalanced in a prior life so that they may be healed and resolved.

For certain, agreeing to an earthly incarnation is a heroic act.

Soul growth takes place over the souls' many lifetimes. Recall that newer souls set out to master survival in the physical world. They then progress to a middle level where they seek success in occupations and avocations, including in relationships with others. Over time, the soul develops compassion and love for others and eventually turns to itself as it deepens its capacity for love.

If you are looking beyond the veneer of day-to-day life to understand yourself, your patterns of thought, your feelings and behavior, you are moving toward awakening. This is a signal that the matters of your interior world are next to be mastered. For many lifetimes prior, you have looked outward, consumed by both the pleasures and problems of the exterior world. With an outward orientation, blame for problems is often projected onto others. As you turn inward and move away from an outward orientation, the question *why is this happening to me* is replaced with a question that will yield deeper growth—*what does my soul hope to achieve from this experience*?

Realizing that you are a soul having a human experience shifts your perspective. It puts you squarely on the path of soul growth. It helps you more quickly identify lessons to be learned and emotional trauma to be healed. It also sets the stage for you to develop more effective coping mechanisms. Removing the residue that has collected from earlier lives is your soul's intention. Once accomplished, you are no longer immobilized by the avalanche of smut that has slowed your soul's maturation.

Further on the road, you will begin to sense the light of your divinity radiating within. Even a glimmer of the radiant light within is good news. On the path back to God, the light shines, enabling you to see that peace and joy are within reach. As an eternal being, you are in the process of evolving spiritually until you fully awaken to your divine essence. This is your soul's destiny.

During sojourns to the interlife, you return to a state of unconditional acceptance and love. You regain the memory of all that you are and all that you have experienced from the moment of your individuation. As you gain wisdom from life's myriad lessons, your soul matures. As you grow spiritually, you are more ready and able to begin the more complicated lessons of love. Key to maturation is your deepening capacity to love.

Earlier on, your soul set out on your individual path ready to experience life in its many forms. From the early days of separation from the Creator Source, you were aware that something was missing. You longed to find it and have spent many lifetimes trying to fill the yearning through acquisition, conquest, and achievement. You may have even taken a detour and hovered in darkness instead.

Finally, you will reach a point when you realize that the yearning cannot be satiated externally. You will understand that it only can be found within. Satisfying this desire will only be filled once you have acquired the wisdom of love.

Awakening to love is a complicated and lengthy process. It entails understanding every aspect of love and bringing each into balance.

The image of a Rubik's Cube comes to mind. When it's new, the colors are perfectly lined-up, like the purity of the soul at its moment of individuation. I imagine the turns to the cube as different lifetimes. It only takes a few turns, a few lifetimes, before the original perfection is obscured. For most of us, returning the Cube to its original order is an exhaustive process. Some of us give up, concluding that only a select few can accomplish the goal.

Unlike solving the Rubik's Cube, all of us are destined to master love. Although we set our individual pace, each of us is assured of awakening to our divine essence. Endlessly patient, God is waiting.

Relationships are laboratories of the spirit. They are hospitals of the soul. They are the places where the wounds that we hold will be brought up, because that's the only way they can be healed.

—MARIANNE WILLIAMSON

2

The Role of Relationships in the Soul's Growth

From the moment of birth in each life, you are embedded in relationships that shape your experience of life. You learn about life and how to live in this complicated world through your relationships with others. In your earliest days, this learning is localized with your parents. As you grow, your instructor-pool expands to include siblings, other relatives, neighbors, teachers, religious figures, friends, co-workers, partners, and your fellow global citizens.

Similarly, your soul learns in relationships with others. Through human interactions and experiences, your soul learns the lessons you embedded within your life plan. In addition to what you hope to learn in an incarnation, you may have incorporated other objectives in your life plan, including healing, balancing, or serving others.

It is a rare soul plan that can be achieved by a person living an isolated and solitary life. Most common, the soul sets out to accomplish the goals embedded within its life plan with members of its soul family. Interactions between personalities give rise to transformation in the same way that combining two chemicals produces a changed element.

You are the casting director as well as the star, screen writer and director of the metaphorical play that is your upcoming life. Once you have defined the goals of your upcoming incarnation and major parameters, you begin the process of identifying soul family members to cast in certain roles.

An important part of the planning discussions are the negotiations that take place to secure the agreement of soul intimates to assume key roles.

This process is not one sided. Although, occasionally, souls selflessly agree to put their own plans on hold to assume a specific role in the next incarnation; more often, there is a matching of life plan objectives that meets the needs of both souls.

The wisdom, healing, and balance we seek is embedded in relationship challenges. Often, this precludes "happily ever after." Spiritual regression case study research has taught us that upheaval motivates. Contrast, opposition, and duality are indeed effective teachers. In fact, the absence of something, often is behind the motivation to find it.

All agreements are made from the eternal love that binds soul family members. While this might seem obvious, it becomes somewhat more difficult to understand when the role that is assumed in the life is far from enhancing and may be downright toxic.

The importance of a soul plan relationship is not correlated with its duration. Souls regularly agree to assume important roles for each other even when the life relationship is not long lasting. Some obvious examples include inspiring teachers who leave indelible marks on your life and partners who die or depart after brief relationships. While humans are challenged and saddened by relationships that end, souls happily move on when the agreed upon objective has been accomplished.

The soul's mission is to deepen its capacity for love. It carries this out by learning to give love, to receive love, and more succinctly—to be love.

The first five clients introduced here illustrate the important roles that relationships, whether parents, siblings, spouses, lovers, or friends, play in spiritual growth and the long process of awakening.

A point about the process bears elaboration. In past life regression, some individuals return to a single life, while others revisit multiple lifetimes. In the latter instances, the transitions can seem abrupt, and the details accessed about each lifetime may be limited. What unfolds through these snapshots, however, is incredibly invaluable when long held beliefs, feelings, and coping behaviors are spotlighted and patterns identified. These give the session therapeutic value and provide directionality for the client's future work.

* * *

You are first introduced to Vera. In this case, you see how her higher self guided us through multiple lifetimes in a single regression session to highlight a pattern of beliefs that has been shaped and reinforced through many lifetimes. Through Vera's experience, the role parents assume in the unfolding of a soul's plan is highlighted.

VERA

Vera originally scheduled a spiritual counseling session, subsequently choosing to have a past life regression to uncover the origin of limiting beliefs. Her friend who referred her was growing concerned that she was slipping into a depression.

Vera is a 22-year-old college student majoring in biology. She attributed her overall malaise to an inability to cope with parental expectations and to execute independent decisions regarding her future.

Vera's pursuit of a professional career over a traditional marriage was the source of growing family disharmony. Her internal struggle was exacerbated by her cultural conditioning that respecting her parents' wishes should trump her own. She was immobilized by the pressure exerted by her parents, thereby running the risk of losing a prestigious scholarship.

Vera attributed her low self-esteem to several stated beliefs: *I don't know what's best for myself, I don't count, I'm worthless, and I don't deserve.* To break free from the powerlessness that griped her and to begin the hard work of establishing and reinforcing new beliefs, she needed to uncover the origin of these negative beliefs. Her past life regression served as the vehicle.

Vera regresses to a life in 10 BC as a young woman of nineteen years. She lives with her parents and two younger siblings in a small, cave dwelling community near the edge of a forest. Her family survives by hunting and growing small crops. Well past traditional marriage age of 14, she assumes caretaking responsibilities for her siblings and ill mother, along with helping out the villagers. She has a strong sense of duty and obligation. Despite her caretaking, it is not clear that everyone appreciates her efforts. Social norms lead her father to refuse to allow her to hunt with the men, despite her strong wishes.

I want to prove to my dad that I can do things on my own. I need to prove that I have value. I love my siblings. I will do anything to take care of them. I like to make other people be happy, so I don't mind helping.

Upon prompting to go to the next most significant scene in this life, Vera instead moves ahead to a life in the mid-twentieth century. Her father is absent, and her mother supports her and her younger sister by *pleasing men.* Because her mother's profession is well known in the community, Vera is taunted by her schoolmates.

Others are judging me. I feel belittled. They don't bother to get to know me. It's not fair. I hide what my mom does from my little sister to protect her. I feel like I have to help her. I want her to have a good life. I don't hate my mom. I just want the best for my little sister.

The next time Vera is prompted to move ahead, she revisits a third life as a 21-year-old living in London. She works sporadically as a waitress and hangs out with friends. Since leaving her parents' home at 19, she has lived in the streets and bounced around, temporarily staying with friends. She describes a childhood and youth with parents who were not emotionally supportive.

My mom and dad told me that I didn't care about myself, that I wasn't pretty, and that I was stupid. They didn't hold success up as reachable. They were very religious and strict; I didn't like it. I am more of a free spirit. My parents did not like that they couldn't control me.

I only make minimum wage. I hate people knowing that I am just skimming by. I know I want more in life, I have tried so hard. For the past year, I have been living with my boyfriend. He takes care of me. He wants to be with me despite what I am—just a waitress. Despite everything I have said about myself, he wants the best for me. He cares. He tells me that I need to not use the past to judge myself. I want to believe that I can do it, that I can succeed in life.

I feel so insecure, but my boyfriend tells me I am worthy of being loved. I feel like I need to learn how to love myself, and then I will be able to accept the love I receive. But it's hard because the main people I want to love me, my parents, won't speak to me.

Vera identifies them as her parents in the current life.

She moves ahead in that life to age 25 and sees herself at a party. She is distressed because she and her boyfriend have broken-up.

It was for the best. I was bringing him down. He wanted to marry me. I never believed in myself. I was drinking a lot, and I realized that the alcohol was tasting funny. No one would take me home. This guy was following me around. He raped me. I tried to fight him off, but I couldn't. He choked me. He left me and didn't even know that I was dead.

Vera moves up and out of her body, moving to the most distant of the four lives her higher self has selected for review. In it, we meet Amara, living more than 2500 years ago. As a young girl of 10-years-old, she was subjected to a spiritual ritual in which she was sexually violated. Her parents who were members of the religious group allowed this to happen.

I didn't feel like it was okay, despite being told that it was. After it happened, I was treated badly by the people in the village. I was ostracized. My family blamed me, telling me it was my fault. No one blamed the man. I was cast out of the village. I had to prove that I could take care of myself. It was hard, I was only a young girl. I didn't live long before I died.

Vera reexperienced four lifetimes, seeing in each of them that she was badly mistreated and rejected, including by her parents who reinforced beliefs of worthlessness and set limiting expectations. Judgement by others loomed large. Desperate to seek their love and approval, she learned to suppress her own desires and dreams, to prioritize the desires of others.

In soul state, she learned that there were many other lifetimes in which she suffered repeating patterns of mistreatment. Each of these further shattered her sense of value and worth and reinforced ideas that she was neither capable nor deserving of happiness and success. In the plan her soul crafted for this current lifetime, Vera heroically decided that she would surface these falsely framed beliefs in order for them to be dispelled and replaced. In doing so, she seeded the upheaval that would cause her to confront and hopefully replace wrongly held beliefs.

Just as her soul planned, discontent had forced Vera to challenge her parents' strongly asserted views, including their discouragement of her dreams and ambitions. Their own strong opinions and traditions had seeded doubts. In prior lives, the views of others overpowered her inner knowing of what was in her best interest. Not surprisingly, prior to her regression work, she stated that she didn't know what was best for herself.

Uncovering the origin of her beliefs, carried across 2500 years and reinforced in multiple lives, has empowered Vera. Applying this insight has helped her to confront limiting beliefs and free herself from the negative emotions they elicited. She has stopped criticizing herself, and instead began formulating new beliefs about her capacity to succeed and lead a happy and joy filled life. Unburdened of the weight of past mistreatment and relieved of the baggage of false beliefs, Vera's days are now filled with more delight. While her parents' behavior has not changed, she now no longer believes that respecting their desires for her life is more important than respecting her own.

* * *

The next case introduces us to Miquel, whose challenges in life began in early childhood. Once regressed, he engaged with several spirit guides who offered insights and healing.

MIQUEL

Miquel is a 45-year-old architect who is married with twin boys who are 18 months old. His wife and children are the center of his world. He described a very unhappy childhood due to his *dysfunctional* birth family and still carries the emotional scars. His low self-esteem is reflected in a lack of self-confidence and feelings of incompetence. His low self-worth is in contrast to his apparent professional success and his current loving and joy filled family life.

Miquel's story is a great example of our higher self capturing our attention. Perhaps something similar has happened to you.

After attending a multi-day workshop at my center, I added Miquel to the distribution list for our electronic calendar of events. Five years later, he had yet to attend another event but never deleted himself from the mailing list. Sitting at his computer a day after learning that his mother had terminal cancer, he received a notice of an upcoming event. By then, the news of his mother's imminent death had put him in crisis. Oddly, after deleting the event notice, it reappeared—dozens of times the same day.

Puzzled, but curious, he decided it was a sign that it would be best to follow. He later noted that attending the event changed his life.

Several months after his mother's death, he scheduled a regression, hoping to understand the purpose of his birth family's dysfunction and the negative impact it had on his sense of self. Despite all of the past acrimony, he still hoped that he might reconcile with his siblings.

Miquel recalled a chaotic and frightening childhood, resulting from his mother's alcoholism and bipolar condition. When intoxicated, she would become verbally and physically abusive. The situation was so extreme that for many years, he feared for the family's collective safety.

> *She would become a raging lunatic, constantly striking fear in the family and pitting family members against each other.*

His mother's outbursts were so unpredictable that over time, Miquel stopped inviting friends over to the house. He disconnected from all of his childhood friends, unable to handle the shame. His social isolation added to his low self-esteem.

Miquel's father traveled for business and was described as *checked-out.* After his parents divorced, more than twenty years ago, Miguel's contact with him has been limited.

Miquel had three sisters, the oldest died of a drug overdose in her early twenties. The other two, much closer in age, have been close friends and, despite, or perhaps because of, their mother's illness, they had been very protective of her. Through childhood and into the present, the sisters would gang-up and bully Miquel. To this day, Miquel is singled out as the problem sibling.

Their list of grievances is ever-growing.

One of his sisters is intermittently supportive, although it was decades before she acknowledged their mother's abuse. His other sister continues to deny the abuse and claims that Miquel has overdramatized what she considers normal behavior.

Incessant judging by his mother and sisters has left Miquel feeling like he is often *on trial.*

> *For as long as I can remember, no matter what goes wrong, it's always my fault. I have been and remain the family scapegoat.*

His desire to understand family patterns and use this insight to repair frayed relationships prompted his decision to pursue spiritual regression. Once in a hypnotic trance, Miquel finds himself in a vast, open space that radiates a brilliant white light.

> *It is incredibly peaceful. It goes on forever—into infinity. It has always been there. As I float in this space and look back, my life with my wife and sons feels like an illusion. Now, I feel as I am one with the light. I feel wonderful. If it is possible, I would choose to come back to this space.*
>
> *They are showing me that our eternal nature is peaceful. By contrast, I see my life as this dark, cramped hallway. The contrast between my life and the light and love in the vast expanse is so dramatic.*

Miquel's attention is drawn to two famous paintings, Munch's "The Scream" and Botticelli's "Allegory of Spring."

The one with the lady feels peaceful and nourishing. The one with the scream reflects the dark side of everything. It's very scary.

Miquel's awareness expands to include the previously unnoticed spirit guides who joined him.

They want me to understand. These paintings represent two sides of a coin. And they are both there. The Scream represents my first forty-five years. Botticelli's painting represents the happiness I will have in the second phase of my life.

The coin also represents my life. I see the coin flipping around. One side leads to the other. The first half of my life is the one side of the coin and the second half of my life is the other side of the coin.

I am being shown this to heal me. I see my sons, they are smiling and laughing. They are ushering in joy in the second phase of my life.

Miquel perceives that the birth of the twins was a miracle, coming ten years after he and his wife began trying to have a child. It was both a turn of the coin and a raining down of life. The boys will bring much happiness and give direction to his life in both the immediate and long term. He realizes immediately the profundity of this experience.

During the counseling session that followed, Miquel shared his understanding of the message conveyed by his spirit guides.

The boys' loving glances remind me that I am complete and perfect the way I am. Even though I was hoping to get some understanding as to how to fix my birth family, I see that the spirit guides didn't want me to focus on that at the present. The session was about me. It was a message to prioritize myself.

I feel different. I am less anxious about the family stuff. Even though I don't want to walk away from them, I see that repairing that damage must wait. I saw clearly that the first half of my life is over, and the second half will be a lot better.

Like many, Miquel's childhood scars left him craving love and attention that was not available, given the character and temperaments of his mother and sisters. It is uncertain whether his family members will ever respond differently or convey love and acceptance. Regardless, he is free to choose peace and happiness, to delight in the love and joy that he shares with his wife and sons. He has been reminded that he must look to himself for the affirmation and acceptance that his birth family could not provide.

The birth of the twins marked a turning point in Miquel's life, the beginning of a new phase. Despite his own doubt and early reservations, he has discovered that he is a great father, happily showering his boys with love, affection, and attention. He now sees that these are things he can gift himself. The adoring smiles of his boys has affirmed what his eternal soul knows—he himself is a brilliant spark of divine light.

The healing session provided by the spirit guides lifted residue from decades of emotional neglect and abuse by challenged parents and competitive siblings. It provided Miquel with the tools that he will need to fully comprehend over time how, in their own misdirected ways, they too were grasping for love and attention.

Getting the answers to the questions proved secondary to being bathed in healing light and love. Miquel was the focus of his session, as he should be in life. He can offer himself peace, comfort, love, and acceptance even if it is never available from birth family members.

The infusion of healing light and love by the spirit guides, coupled with the images of his happy, adoring twins, helped Miquel to shift focus. As he did, he immediately felt peace and joy. No longer distracted by the messages of others, he now can hear the whispers of his own soul; reminders that he is whole and complete, and that joy, peace, and happiness are his eternal birth right.

* * *

In the section that follows we meet Jacob. His relationships with his wife and previous romantic partners have challenged him. He now understands that the interpersonal problems he has struggled with offer him opportunities to grow spiritually. Rather than wonder why this has been a pattern for some time, he is looking to understand what his soul hopes to gain through these challenges.

JACOB

Jacob is a 52-year-old married high school principal. He contacted me after reading *Wisdom of Souls* to schedule life between lives hypnotherapy.

His regression sessions were enriched by the many insights he had about himself and their interplay in important relationships.

Jacob discussed marital challenges, which he attributed to his wife's judgmental and harsh attitude. These contribute to a sense that he is not good enough. He has come to realize, given the therapeutic work he has done previously, that his inexperience and discomfort with emotions have played a role in their less than happy marriage.

> *Until a few years ago, I thought the answers to problems were outside myself. I realize now that it is more complicated.*
>
> *Until I was in my 40s, I blamed my parents for their neglect and not protecting me. I believed that my childhood experiences left me lacking a solid foundation.*
>
> *Through the years, mates have described me as emotionally unavailable and commented on what they label as my low affect. I would describe myself as stoic and in control of emotions because I am good at coping with and repressing them.*
>
> *In marrying my wife, I see that I created a challenging emotional environment to navigate. We have so much to learn from each other, including how to deepen and refine love. We don't communicate very well, and I feel responsible. I want to do my part to make it work.*
>
> *At present, I am focused on how I practice love and what is to be my contribution to humanity. I sense I will need courage to take myself beyond my comfort zone.*
>
> *I am shy, meek, and quiet. And I do see how my limiting beliefs about myself play a role, including eroding my self-confidence.*

In the journey to the afterlife that followed, Jacob would gain additional insights that would prove invaluable to his continued emotional and spiritual growth.

Once in deep trance, Jacob reaches the interlife, where he is welcomed by his long-time spirit guide Otis. They have been working together for most of Jacob's 43 lives. Otis is happy to elaborate on Jacob's experience through these lifetimes.

Jacob's soul plan is focused on love, love of self and love for others. Such a plan creates an opportunity for the soul to reach the highest level possible. It includes the full gamut of love—understanding, experiencing, and expressing it. It also includes understanding the limits of love. Once the soul prioritizes love as a goal, it's capacity to give and receive love is deepened and refined over time. Doing so is foundational for spiritual advancement.

If the essence of love is not properly configured before it is expressed, then it will not be received with the intent that it was given. People's capacity for this varies at any one moment in time.

As the regression continues, Otis continues to elaborate on particular aspects of love and their importance for Jacob's development. He shares that one of the stumbling blocks that Jacob has been working to overcome is his analytical approach to love.

Jacob is trying to build his capacity for love, including the love of others and himself. He is trying to figure out what it all means, how it is expressed. This is internal to the soul. Until recently, he has been focused on understanding. More recently, he is focused on implementing what he has learned, quite frankly, through a process of trial and error.

His plan is to learn to optimize love. Despite all the distractions, he is placing a lot of attention on this.

He should continue on as he has been doing. It looks as if his focus is on the right place. The lens is wide open. He is taking in a lot of new information, to refine and practice better. It's awesome.

Jacob's analytical approach on the matter of love predates this lifetime.

Jacob's job in the afterlife includes analyzing the progress made by souls in order to determine the lessons that will need to be embed in future lives. He has been focused on drawing connections between other souls in the interlife and their interactions in human life.

As he formulated his own plan for this lifetime, he decided that he wanted to reach the next level. And so, it follows that he was willing to take on a challenging life to accomplish this.

Otis selected Jacob's cat Carmen to emphasize his point that love is animated and cannot be left only for theoretical understanding, adding that love can be optimized with any other spirit. Jacob instantaneously reacted to the mention of his beloved pet. For several minutes, he swooned as he recalled the joy of the love that they share.

Their relationship in this current life is an example of love that is close to perfect love. Their relationship lacks the complexity of a relationship with another human. Like Jacob, most pet lovers can identify with overwhelming feelings of unconditional love and acceptance that they have with their pets. Most often, these relationships are not encumbered with high or mismatched expectations; nor are they polluted with lots of irrelevant emotions.

On the broader range of emotions that have challenged Jacob in the past, Otis offers encouraging feedback.

Jacob is running toward emotions, not away from them as others have characterized. His wife is creating an opportunity for him to deepen his understanding about emotions, to be more agile.

Their relationship has been orchestrated to challenge him in this regard. This is the role his wife agreed to play, although Jacob feels like she is overplaying the role. For him, it feels somewhat analogous to being in training camp, preparing for the big game.

If Jacob can push aside the negativity that muddies his relationship with his wife, he will have a clearer connection to love. He needs to manage all his emotions, including fear of rejection and any others that stand in the way. Negative emotions deplete his energy. As he manages them better, the energetic vibration of love will emerge more.

Others also agreed to help him expand his emotional capacity during this lifetime.

Jacob is becoming more aware that when he interacts with others, love is the answer, love is the response, love is the main ingredient in the formula. It is encouraging him to interact and respond within the framework of love.

Jacob chose a challenging life plan, including scripting parents who had low emotional abilities. Emotions weren't displayed or taught; neither was how to manage them. This created the opportunity for him to set his own course. The environment frustrated him. But his struggles motivated him to eventually learn how to navigate his emotions.

Love is the keystone of all emotions. It is the end result of dozens of emotions. For Jacob, joy and happiness are supporting emotions. But there are others that hamper it, and so they must be managed in a way that love can surface and be nourished.

As he offers Jacob these important insights about love, Otis gifts all of us with a deeper understanding of love. These lessons on love resonate for humanity as a whole.

The perfection of love is not static. It must be continually practiced to be sustained. Love is a practice. When love is practiced, it becomes more natural.

Souls have a good sense of what love is when they perceive it, even though humans may be perplexed by it. Love is not just an emotion, although emotion is a part of it. Love is an essence that is experienced. It's a combination of concepts, feelings, and emotions.

The challenge humans all across the earth face is to respond with love. The traumas that people endure prevent or block them from this realization. Healing these traumas and learning from them is essential. Later, as they gain more understanding about how this works, they improve. It's a maturation process. As souls mature, responding with love becomes more natural and ingrained. Eventually, the soul reaches the point where it has become enlightened, knowing that love is the answer.

Emotions are the language of the soul. Whatever the emotions experienced, you have to determine whether they are obscuring love or helping to manifest love. Successfully managing emotions that get in the way, for example fear or doubt, allows love to emerge.

Love becomes more prevalent when people deenergize negative emotions.

Fear is generally the opposite of love. As fear is stripped away, love can emerge. The balance of fear versus love applies to every soul. As fear can be shed, love can emerge stronger.

As the conversation about love draws to a close, Otis signals that it is time to escort Jacob to meet with the council of elders, the senior spiritual advisors who are working with him.

Jacob's council includes five beings. They acknowledge his hard work and are pleased with the progress he has made implementing his plan. Their comments and tone offer encouragement. Their unconditional love and acceptance become yet another gift of Jacob's journey into the interlife.

They encourage him to take life one day at a time, to pace himself.

There are no significant obstacles that are beyond your handling. Any limitations that you experience are self-imposed. Suffering is not fuel; it is baggage. At the point where any struggle becomes unproductive or generates more suffering, managing the suffering should take priority.

Before the end of Jacob's session, Otis and Jacob make a brief visit to what Otis labels the council headquarters, in a higher astral realm, to explore the ascension process. Otis counsels that this is a place for higher beings who have progressed.

All lives offer an opportunity to love more consistently and consciously. Over time, they progress further and further toward the perfection of love. Each life is a stepping-stone on the path to a master's level of love. The higher realms are reserved for souls who have consistently manifested love. Perfecting love is a ladder to these higher states of bliss.

Despite its brevity, this stop will serve to inspire and motivate. As he works to fully realize the lessons from his interlife journey, the beauty and the power of the love experienced there will remain a beacon.

Jacob's session not only provided insight about the practical problems of life that he was seeking, but it also enlivened his spiritual quest.

In a follow-up session several months after his LBL, he noted that the session increased his self-confidence. Otis' insights helped him integrate seemingly disparate ideas that he struggled to reconcile. Otis' guidance also affirmed many of Jacob's ideas on spiritual development.

Jacob was excited to share that restarting his meditation practice had become a top priority. Most significant of all was the over-arching message of the experience that he summed up in six words.

My goal is to be love.

Jacob's journey has brought him to a point of great clarity. In turning inward, he has been reminded of great spiritual truths. At our core, we are beings of pure love who journey through many lifetimes on a quest to remember to be and experience the love that is our divine essence.

* * *

In the next case, we will meet Sharon. Like Jacob, her marriage partner assumes a starring role. What is different in her case is that she has agreed to assume a role of service for her husband, who is a member of her soul family. The soul agreement they made provides fertile ground for the spiritual growth they individually hope to achieve. Unlike Jacob, the duration of their agreement was limited to accomplishing the objectives of their plans. To provide contrast, a second member of Sharon's soul family is also playing a key role in the plan her soul hopes to accomplish.

SHARON

Sharon is a 48-year-old tennis instructor with two college-age children. She is on the brink of separating from her husband Robert of 23-years. Despite a tumultuous last six years, including individual and couples counseling, she has been *unable to let the marriage go.*

Several years ago, Sharon began studying eastern spirituality. In a class she met Brian, a kindred spirit who shares this interest. Over time, their connection deepened. Although not romantically or sexually involved, the intensity of their relationship has left them both *feeling like there is a soul connection.*

Sharon scheduled her session hoping to gain insight into her inability to end her troubled marriage and to understand the nature of her connection to Brian.

Once regressed, Sharon finds her energy body floating in the astral realm. Her surroundings are unfamiliar. She connects to a higher being who is named Ariel.

Ariel tells Sharon to trust the spiritual path that she is on.

> *Don't be afraid or get discouraged. Be open to all possibilities. Have faith and keep going. Seek the highest path. Trust the path.*

Ariel understands the pain that Sharon has experienced in her marriage and explains its significance. She confirms that in soul state she and Robert agreed to assume roles that would help their spiritual growth, noting that they share an eternal bond of love which has manifested in different ways in different lifetimes.

> *You have been married to your husband Robert in earlier lives, as well as being siblings. In this lifetime, romantic love is not what unites you. You made this decision knowing that it would be a sacrifice to not share romantic love with him. You have chosen to be of service to him by helping him to mature spiritually.*
>
> *The antagonistic role Robert is playing has led you to fear being judged for your spiritual pursuits. He agreed to assume this role to help you grow.*
>
> *You fear change. You dread hurting your children. Both have prevented you from leaving him. You are reticent to repeat the cycle that led his parents to divorce. But your work may be done with him. Leaving him may be more helpful to his soul's development.*

Ariel reminds Sharon that her plan to remain married to Robert for their lifetimes can be modified. Despite all reservations and her love for Robert, Sharon knows deep down that neither of them is being served by the slow death of their marriage.

With the hope of brokering resolution, I call in Robert's higher self to hear directly from him and ask him to share his view of the plan they made in soul state. Sobbing, he is remorseful as he speaks to Sharon.

I hurt you. I was wrong to hurt you. I neglected you and took you for granted. I tried to control you. I'm so sorry. It doesn't have to be like this now. I love you, but I can't hold you. You are free to go. I know that you are done.

Equally emotional, Sharon's higher self tells Robert's that she too is sorry, but that she has to move on. Both are still crying when Robert finally departs. Sharon's higher self chooses this time to offer her own view on the decisions Sharon is facing.

Sharon is in touch with her divine essence. In an earlier life as a monastic, she connected to her divinity through nature. She agreed to the plan with Robert in order to help him realize his own divinity. But she needs to leave Robert. She won't suffer. I have plans for her to help others to grow spiritually, including the people with whom she works. They bring out the best in her.

Sharon's higher self elaborates on what might best be understood as a mid-life contingency soul plan.

Her friend Brian is another soul who is working to grow and become a better person. He surfaced in Sharon's life because of his own marital struggles and the need for his soul to connect to her.

Because of the romantic chemistry that the two enjoyed in earlier lives, she feels connected to him. Their lifetimes together were very happy. She knew it would be difficult to spend a lifetime apart because their hearts are connected in this special way. Knowing that they would be romantically involved again in a future lifetime was enough.

In this life, she is focused on helping herself and others grow spiritually.

The discussion about Brian results in the spontaneous appearance of his higher self who is confused about how to handle his desire to be with Sharon and his commitment to his wife. He wants to do the right thing, but he admits that *it's hard.*

Admittedly, their respective struggles to resolve their marital problems have been encumbered by their emotional draw to each other. Despite their eternal bond of love, the two have both been working hard to do the right thing in their marriages. Sadly, this has left them frustrated in unsatisfying marriages without the depth of connection that they have enjoyed in prior lifetimes.

Sharon's higher self acknowledges that now that she and her husband have reached a decision point, she will be in a position to patiently wait to see how Brian resolves his situation.

Once again, we hear from her higher self.

> *Waiting leaves her vulnerable. But it is okay, she doesn't have to be the strong one all the time. Relationships are reciprocal. They go two ways. She doesn't like to be the weak one. She will have to learn that it will be okay. She needs to let others be the strong one.*

These last words trigger an emotional response from both Brian and Sharon. Both are crying. Brian is the first to break the silence.

> *I'm so sorry. I am going to shut it down. I am going to will myself to resist Sharon.*

No certainty or closure is possible at this moment.

In the presence of the higher beings, the souls of Sharon and Brian embrace. Linked by their eternal bond, they are cradled in the loving embrace of the higher beings. They are encouraged to love themselves, even when they don't live-up to their own high standards. Most importantly, they are reminded that their feelings are an outgrowth of their eternal bond.

Brought up from trance, Sharon voices surprise that the session was much more emotional than she expected.

Sharon shares that her direct connection to her husband's higher self was a welcome change from the negativity he projects and the critical nature of his personality. She is at peace with the need to end their marriage and pleased that her higher self has helped her make such a difficult choice.

Despite the uncertainty of how her relationship with Brian might evolve, she is calm knowing that their loving bond transcends both time and place.

A year after her session, Sharon informed me that she had filed for divorce and moved with her children. Reaching the decision had taken six years, but she now has decades ahead to reap the benefits. As for Brian, he remains with his wife. What remains uncertain is whether the soul agreement that Sharon and Brian made is completed or whether there are other chapters that will unfold in this lifetime.

Those who live in societies in which there is great freedom to exercise free will can gain a false sense of control over life. As most have learned, often painfully, having the freedom to choose does not assure positive or happy outcomes. People struggle with various human problems, stuck between choices that seem untenable. Even those working to accomplish a long-term goal are limited in their event horizons.

These limitations are not shared by the soul.

There is tremendous relief once a problem is viewed from the perspective of the higher self. Viewing your difficulties within the context of your soul's plan can free you from buyer's remorse.

In Sharon's case, learning from her higher self that she had completed the soul agreement she made with Robert freed her to make a decision on which she vacillated for six years. Understanding the context of her feelings for Brian spared her from self-recrimination.

Knowing that both of them are members of her soul family, who agree time and again to incarnate together for mutual spiritual growth, eased her acceptance of life disappointments that might otherwise have been overwhelming. Now, with the understanding of their spiritual bonds, she is able to find the peace that had been so elusive.

* * *

We are next introduced to Kelly, who through her regression experience learned how a long-standing pattern of belief and behavior left her prioritizing the needs of others, at great expense to her own well-being and spiritual growth. Her desire to understand relationship challenges with her first husband, family members, and friends drew attention to underlying feelings of low self-worth and a compensating tendency to put others first. Through her experience, we learn that the need for balance is critical, including positive qualities such as kindness and compassion. We also find encouragement that seemingly intractable patterns can be broken.

Kelly

Kelly is a 55-year-old who had a happy childhood growing up in a large, loving nuclear family. She has two adult sons and one daughter by her first husband. They divorced after 14 years when she fell in love with Dennis. She described the first time she met him at a neighborhood swimming pool as if she *had been struck with a bolt of lightning.* After 13 years of guilt and angst, made worse by the opinions of family members, Kelly and Dennis married.

Currently, Kelly is co-owner of a day spa, which has left her with little time to pursue other interests and passions. She has been contemplating the sale of her half of the business but is worried about the impact on her long-time partner and close friend. She is mindful that putting her own interests first is a factor and recurring challenge.

Kelly scheduled life between lives hypnotherapy with hope of gaining insight as to what her soul wished to accomplish through several important relationships, and to better understand the guilt she carries for having divorced her first husband to partner with Dennis. She was also hoping to gain insight into why she struggles emotionally to prioritize herself over others. This pattern too often leaves her feeling trapped, in addition to feeling guilty when she prioritizes herself over the needs or desires of others.

During a past life regression, she revisits a life during the early 20th century in London that sets the stage for a key relationship in her current life. Her name is Margaret, and she has been widowed when her husband went to serve in World War I. She was forced to be strong because so many were losing their loved ones because of the war.

Amidst the misery, suffering, and death of the war, people clung to the limited happiness that they could find. One way they coped was to *live life in the moment.*

Like many others, Margaret believed that each of us only has one true love. What happened after her husband's death shattered the certainty she had about who and how we love.

Shortly after her husband's death, Margaret fell madly in love with another man. Social pressures necessitated keeping her new relationship with Frederick a secret from her family and friends. They ran off to southern France to shield themselves from family scorn. Sadly, their days of happiness were limited.

I was swept off my feet by Frederick. My feelings for him were overwhelming. The intensity of our relationship left me questioning if the love I had for my husband was real. It was shameful how quickly I recovered from the loss of George. I felt so guilty. I was acting as if he was expendable. But in truth, my relationship with Frederick made it easy for me to recover.

After a blissful year together, her beloved Frederick died in an automobile accident.

Frederick was so smart; wise, in fact. He was adventurous and fun as well as strong. He was irresistible. We snuck around. My relationship was not well received at home. It defied convention.

Kelly later learned upon Margaret's death, years later, that her soul set two intentions for future lifetimes.

The first was that in the future she would live life to the fullest.

I will seize the moment. I will not allow the opinions of others to restrain or constrain me.

The happiness she found after eloping with Frederick convinced her that she was right to go against family and social convention.

The second intention was even more specific.

In a future life I will recreate the intense passion and love that was cut short by Frederick's tragic death!

In soul state, she identifies eternal characteristics. She knows herself as strong, versatile, kind, and loving. She is also aware that these latter two will be defining qualities that will cause her heartache but lead to joy in upcoming incarnations.

Kelly's past life regression session has given direction to her life between lives session and helped her to refine the questions that will guide it. It has also hinted at problem areas that might unfold in future lifetimes. As she will learn, unless the soul's positive eternal characteristics are balanced, they can become an Achilles heel, especially when they collide with the soul's intention for a lifetime.

One month later, Kelly returns for her life between lives session.

Once in trance, she finds herself amidst swirls of purple and green that wrap her in a blanket of peace and love. Soon after, she meets her spirit guide Edward, who she originally knew in a human lifetime many years before. Together, they head to the hall of records. Settling into a large room filled with long tables within a majestic marble temple, Edward wastes no time pointing out the challenges that Kelly faces.

> *Kelly's soul plan includes working to realize her worth and strengthen her personal power. She has been working on both of these issues for 400 lifetimes. Although I think she is making progress, her tendency to undervalue herself and her accomplishments leave her believing otherwise. She's forgotten her potential and that she is special and powerful. She can do whatever she sets out to do.*
>
> *Her prior lifetimes have undercut this view. She has to change her beliefs. Her belief that others are good and that she is bad prompts her to serve them rather than serve herself.*

As Edward continues, we begin to understand why Kelly is having difficulty reveling in the progress she has made.

> *Being overly compassionate, Kelly fell into a trap. She is too sensitive to the needs of others. She believes that she has to earn her value from others. This is why she is stuck in this pattern of putting them first. While her compassion for others is a gift, it has impeded her progress.*
>
> *In her current lifetime, she is working to learn how to honor herself while remaining compassionate—balancing compassion of self and others. She is learning to be more compassionate with herself and know her own power. But she has gone through a lot of pain to do so.*
>
> *She holds a belief that her life has less value than the lives of others. This was reinforced in prior lives, in which she served others as a slave, servant, monk, and*

devotee in various religious orders. She is having difficulty breaking through this belief because of the compounding of experience in these many lives of servitude.

This false belief has not been counterbalanced by the previous lives in which she had high academic achievement, personal power, wealth, and success. They have not been enough to balance compassion for herself and for others against that belief.

In this life, she is learning to serve herself, to break out of the concept of servitude. She gets stuck going along with what others want her to do, believing that others won't love her if she speaks and acts on her truth. This doubt about being loved and accepted for herself originates in a series of lives in which she was mistreated.

Kelly needs to come into her power and know that speaking her truth will not scare away the people who truly love her. In order to neutralize the doubt, she needs to speak up and act on her truth.

Her relationship with her first husband is an example. She didn't follow her heart. Instead, she viewed the relationship in terms of how it would please others. He was considered a great catch by her family and friends. Plus, the timing was considered right for her to settle down and pick a husband.

She and her husband were business partners in a past life. They stuck with the business, despite knowing that it would be best for them to part ways. In this life, the essence of their plan was to be strong enough to part ways, and not to hang onto the marriage partnership beyond the point when it was good for both of them. The ending of their marriage is not a failure, it was not planned to last forever. They brought balance to something that had been left unbalanced.

Kelly is still carrying tremendous guilt about her affair and resulting divorce. Her soul purposely chose to incarnate in a family holding strict religious views. These religious beliefs and family sentiment have amplified her guilt for what they perceive as her transgression. Her remorse was eating away at her already low self-worth.

As her soul made the plan for this lifetime, she intentionally set this dynamic in place. The negative emotions she experienced because of the strongly held views of others placed a spotlight on her pattern of placing others first. Her soul intended to break her long-standing pattern of prioritizing others. In doing so, she is forced to struggle with her own sense of worth.

The extent of compassion she is able to develop for herself reflects the progress she has made.

Edward cautions that while she is increasing her self-worth, it will likely need continued work in the future. He elaborates.

Kelly and Dennis both have low self-worth, which reveals itself in their challenges with money. They are living within an illusion that there is a lack of money.

What is actually going on is a result of their lack of personal power. If they stand more firmly in their personal power, the money will follow. Their low self-worth is displaced through the illusion of lack—that there is not enough. Because they undervalue themselves, they falsely believe that they lack adequate funds.

Edward notes that many other humans are struggling with the same issue.

There is much to learn from Edward's message, which takes on a universal appeal and relevance.

When plans are made in soul state, the soul is detached from the experience of suffering that may result once their plan is implemented on earth. Souls recall that they suffered, but they do not relive the intensity of the emotions that accompanied the suffering. It's like recalling physical pain. You can recall it, but you don't relive it.

In the interlife, beings are in a state of bliss and know that they constantly return to bliss. This mitigates the idea of potential suffering.

In human experience, you need to see beyond the suffering in order to cope with it and to know that everything will be alright. And to learn from the suffering, you need to look for the common themes that are embedded within your suffering. It is hard to do.

Kelly had identified the issues and themes that caused her to suffer in this life. Scheduling her LBL was the step she took in order to uncover the intentions embedded within a soul plan that was causing so much suffering.

Kelly's sensitivity and compassion for others intensified the drama and pain of her affair. Although swept off her feet when she met Dennis, the decision to divorce was not made easily. Following her heart was very difficult. Her husband's behavior, including his revenge, created a living hell. But as her soul hoped when devising her plan, she was able finally to prioritize her own needs.

Edward elaborates on how Kelly's plan continues to unfold.

Luckily, she built other joys into her plan, like her children, to keep her going through the most difficult times. However, even this joy presents another challenge for Kelly. She needs to distance herself emotionally from her first husband while understanding that her children need to cultivate their relationship with their father. The children's relationship with him intensifies the challenge for her, but if she is to accomplish her plan, she needs to break the emotional bond with him.

Kelly's success helps to remind her to love herself. She is worthy of a life of joy. It is strengthening her compassion for herself, breaking the pattern that has challenged her for so many lifetimes. Her sense of personal power is growing, and it will serve her well in the future.

Edward's wisdom underscores an important factor of soul development. Bringing balance to patterns of thinking, emotions, and behaviors can take many lifetimes. Patterns formed and strengthened across lifetimes are not easily broken. If they have been reinforced by trauma, they will be even harder to change. Accomplishing this requires determination, patience, and a willingness to accept setbacks. It can be eased by self-acceptance, self-forgiveness, and self-love.

Before her LBL session ends, Edward escorts her to council members. Their time with her is dedicated to an energetic release and healing which is a perfect complement to the many insights that Edward has already shared.

The council members are emphatic with their words of encouragement regarding the progress she has made on accomplishing her soul's plan.

We want to bolster her confidence. She needs to know that she is doing so well and making progress.

We want her to take time out to enjoy life!

She should not take things so seriously. She should take time out to enjoy. She needs to have confidence in herself to go forward. The specifics of how to maximize this has been shared by Edward. She should follow the advice and direction that her guide has provided her, especially about her worth.

The sense of personal power that Kelly has gained is to be used to help herself as well as others. In the immediate, she can choose to apply it to back out of the business she co-owns and to pursue other interests. Doing so becomes an opportunity to break through the pattern of making choices to please others rather than herself.

Kelly's regression experience provided the answers to the questions she posed. The understanding that she gained about key relationships turned the spotlight back on her. Her spirit guide and council members were emphatic that her propensity for prioritizing others had not merely shortchanged her countless times but had crystalized a pattern that needed shattering. Her sense of worth hangs in the balance, calling her to develop compassion for herself.

Kelly's decision to understand her soul's motivation led her to choose life between lives hypnotherapy. Her resolve to be guided in future choices by the insight embedded within her soul plan and to incorporate the wisdom of the higher beings who support her will serve her well. These decisions don't produce magical results or change. What they do accomplish is securing the highest available counsel to incorporate at future choice-points. Not only is it certain that shaped by this guidance, future decisions will prompt the greatest spiritual growth; but ultimately, those choices will lead to greater peace and joy.

A year after her sessions, Kelly told me that she sold her half of the business and is now happily pursuing a career in real estate. Step by step, she is learning to prioritize her needs and desires.

As communal beings, we spend much of our lives embedded in relationships. These interactions with others provided the framework within which our soul works to accomplish life plans. Crafted in the bond of love that connects soul family members, growth can occur, whether the assumed life roles are supportive or toxic.

Upheaval and pain are strong motivators. Not surprisingly, both are common to human experience. What is less commonly understood is that the soul does not shy away from crafting life plans that may well result in both turmoil and suffering. Through these negative experiences, we are motivated to find the path to peace and joy.

From our earliest moments, the beliefs we hold about ourselves are shaped through the countless exchanges we have with others. Over time, a sense of self is molded. Loving interactions reinforce a positive view of self, while mistreatment detracts. Throughout history, few have escaped experiences which have traumatized in the immediate and left residual scars on the soul. As the soul moves through its cycle of reincarnations, it plans lifetimes to heal earlier damage and reshape the false beliefs that it holds about itself.

Over time, patterns are formed. In some cases, patterns have been so reinforced that they crystalize and risk becoming petrified. The more often a pattern is repeated, the harder it is to break. This includes even seemingly positive patterns, such as a tendency to prioritize others over ourselves and the beliefs propelling them. Beliefs that are out of balance, including those about ourselves, are carried by the soul through time until they are balanced. Balance is a crucial component of spiritual advancement.

If you are looking to understand what lessons you included in your life plan, a good place to start is identifying your patterns of belief, feelings, and behavior. These are clues about the spiritual growth that remains on your journey to deepen your capacity for love.

Loss makes artists of us all
as we weave new patterns in the fabric of our lives.

—GRETA W. CROSBY

3

What Loss Teaches

We not only learn through our day-to-day exchanges with others but often when these relationships end. Loss results from death, divorce, separation, and abandonment. It may also occur when close friends, relatives, or associates are estranged.

Within loss there is the opportunity for growth. Each loss of a loved one offers a chance for us to deepen our capacity for love, which is essential for our spiritual growth.

These words ring shallow for those overcome by the searing pain that too often accompanies loss. The pain that shouts *you took a part of my heart when you left.* Most know from experience that as you navigate your way on the path through grief, it is easy to become disoriented by overwhelming emotions and lose your way.

Given time, most grief dissipates. But when it is immersed in trauma, or you don't recover from a profound loss, the soul carries the damage forward. The process for healing becomes complicated when distorted beliefs are a byproduct.

At the point when the soul seeks resolution for earlier trauma, including profound loss, it makes a life plan that will resurface the unresolved pain and associated beliefs. Often, this manifests in personal dramas that elicit the same emotions. In these instances, the soul hopes for a different outcome. It seeks to heal and balance the emotions while modifying falsely held beliefs.

Recall that your beliefs shape emotions and feelings, which in turn influence your coping mechanisms and behavior. In the cases that follow, you will see how falsely held beliefs and unresolved emotions have cascaded forward in time, embedded in life plans that the soul hopes will achieve needed healing.

* * *

In this first case, we are introduced to Freja, who is betrayed by a relative and close friend, compounded with loss and estrangement from loved ones.

Freja

Freja is 67-year-old writer who emigrated to the United States from Sweden three decades ago. She lived with her aunt and uncle for several years until she married. Initially isolated, over the decades she cultivated several close friendships. She had barely recovered from the death of her beloved aunt and uncle, compounding the loss of her father and sister several years before, when her emotional world was turned upside down.

Several betrayals during the previous months left her confused, angry, and distraught. She was swindled out of an inheritance by a family member and deceived by her best friends.

During an extended visit from Sweden, her mother's actions led to a schism with Freja and her daughter. Against her advice and urging, her mother had encouraged Freja's daughter to move to New York City. Many months had passed since her move and their last conversation, which was a dramatic departure from their previous closeness. Furious and distraught, she sent her mother back to Sweden and had not spoken with her in months. In the ensuing months, Freja's fear for her daughter's safety intensified through each additional day of their falling out.

She scheduled a regression session, following the recommendation of her Reiki practitioner, hoping to understand the loss overwhelming her.

Once in trance, Freja revisited a life as a man whose name is Nils. He lives with his wife and two young boys on their small farm. Farm life is difficult and financial security is far from assured. He finds himself on a main square in Stockholm. The usually crowded square and surrounding streets are deserted. He has come into the city to sell livestock.

We move ahead in time to determine what we are meant to understand about this farmer's life and experiences. We find Nils floating above his body, having just died. His wife and teenage sons, who are at his bedside, are distraught. He realizes that he has never told them how much he loves them, through his veneer of toughness and strength. Unheard by his family, his soul cries out.

I love you. I will love you forever. I am not sure that I can survive without you.

Nils initially chose not to cross over into the afterlife, believing he must stay to protect his family. In fact, he remained earthbound long after his beloved wife crossed, and his sons grew to be old men and died. When he finally reached the interlife, the four had a joyous reunion that had been long delayed. In his decision to remain earthbound, Nils confused love with protection.

In this subsequent incarnation as Freja, Nils' son has reincarnated as her daughter and his beloved spouse has incarnated as her aunt. As in the prior lifetime, her love of both is intense. Through her plan for this lifetime, she is seeking to balance her tendency to confuse love and protection.

We are joined by Freja's spirit guides. They want her to understand and accept that sometimes love brings pain. They know that her heart is heavy because of the betrayal by friends but they want her to put this in perspective. They invite her to step outside any tendency for stubbornness and to shift her focus.

Some people pretend to love, while other love is genuine and lasting. Instead of dwelling on your friends, we want you to focus on the deep and eternal loves that have enriched your life. That is one of the reasons why we have selected Nils' life for you to revisit. Although it wasn't expressed, his love for his family members was enduring.

We want you to learn to love yourself and to revel in the deep and abiding love of those who genuinely love you.

Relationships can teach you how to find love within yourself. Your relationship with your husband is such an example. You feel his negativity is encumbering your efforts to love yourself. We see it differently.

The guides remind Freja that it is possible for the lessons of love to be learned through contrast, although doing so is far more challenging and comes with peril.

Freja is instructed to connect to the energy of her husband and to recall the love that forged their marriage more than two decades ago. She accepts their encouragement to express what weighs on her heart.

Don't protect me too much. You always anticipate that something bad is going to happen. You are always negative. Your fear is overshadowing your love. It overshadows my effort to remain positive.

Prior to this exchange, Freja has not seen this very tendency in herself.

Her grief over the deaths of her father, sister, uncle, and beloved aunt has made her fearful, cautious, and overprotective. As she cries out that she cannot lose anyone else, she is reminded that she too has been grasping to protect those she loves. In doing so, she has put a wedge between both her daughter and mother. Once again confusing love and protection, she has allowed her fears to dominate.

With the help of her guides, Freja is shown how her fears have overshadowed more positive expressions of love. Like her husband's overprotectiveness, her own pushed her daughter and mother away.

Freja is encouraged to connect to her daughter's energy and to feel the intensity of the love she has for her.

By revisiting Nil's life, she has experienced first-hand how the bonds of love are not broken or lost in death. Loving connections transcend the limits of time.

In addition to the lessons on balance, love, and self-love, she has received comfort, release, and insight. By guiding her back through time and peering into an earlier life, Freja has been readied to refine and expand her capacity for love.

Lacking upheaval, the human tendency is to lean toward complacency. Upheaval often brings needed change into the light of day. From our human perspective, upheaval is dreaded and barely tolerated. But from the soul's perspective, upheaval prompts growth, so it is a good thing. Because the soul is confident that we will trudge through adversity and come out stronger, it is not reticent about negotiating with members of its soul family to instigate upheaval.

One of the challenges of being a soul having a human experience is uncovering the master plan. The best way to do this is to back far enough away from the turmoil in your life to be able to see clearly what purpose it serves.

In the midst of upheaval, the best question to ask yourself is what did my soul hope to gain by including this in my life plan? Although you may not like what you have to cope with, finding out how it eventually serves you may ease the pain.

* * *

In the next case, we meet Samantha. Like many, the death of her beloved spouse raised questions about life after death. Her search for answers led her to schedule a spiritual regression session. Not only did she get the answers to her questions, but the lessons were presented in a way she could have never dreamed.

SAMANTHA

Samantha is a 54-year-old department store buyer who has two adult sons. Her husband Peter died a year ago after battling cancer for years. They had been married for 30 years. The three years following his diagnosis were an emotional roller coaster, during which she immersed herself in researching the illness and potential treatments, hoping to change the grim prognosis.

Samantha's grief propelled her search for evidence of life after death.

I have been living with death for a very long time. I am searching and hoping to discover that there is more than 'nothing' after we die. I was raised in a religion that offered no belief in an afterlife. I am open minded but skeptical.

Before Peter's death, Samantha had an out-of-body experience, in which she found herself engulfed in a beautiful white light. In what she labeled as a spontaneous experience of the vastness of existence, she was embraced in the loving comfort of deceased family members. She considered it a gift and knew that it helped sustain her through her husband's final days.

After Peter's death, Samantha sought counsel from others in an effort to answer the questions she had about what lies beyond physical life. She had sessions with mediums but remained skeptical. After reading the testimonies of those who had near-death experiences, she joined an NDE support group. Despite all of this, she remained cynical.

Samantha's scheduling of a transpersonal session was not surprising, given the extent of her exploration. It was a logical next step in her search. Like others before her who came in similar search, I cautioned that her guides might not be inclined to offer-up proof of God. Caution aside, she excitedly approached her regression session.

Samantha easily moved into trance and sensed that she was a woman wrapped in soft robe that was smooth and silky. She described floating in a comfortable emptiness initially, but as the scene changed, she found herself floating among the stars. Alone at first, she was joined by several white swans. The swans began communicating telepathically.

They are saying it's okay, it's okay, whoever they are, they are saying it's okay. I want to cry for some reason. They are beckoning to me. Sssh, sssh… you did the best you could.

No, I didn't!

Wrapped in their massive wings, Samantha allowed them to comfort her, experiencing their embrace as pure joy. For several minutes, she remained engulfed in this loving hold before they resumed communicating.

They seem to know me pretty well. They keep repeating, stop beating yourself up.

Now they are repeating, love, love, love. They really want me to believe that it is okay.

I am telling them what I did wrong. I did this, I did this. How can it be okay?

They are repeating another point. Love, love, love… that's what you gave, that's who you were.

They are trying to show me that someone wants to talk to me. I don't want to see—they are telling me that I am too much of a judge. It is my Achilles heel. I judge myself too harshly.

Distraught and crying, Samantha was unmoved by their words of comfort and acceptance. Several minutes passed before she was able to regain calm. As the scene shifted before her, so did her emotions as she recognized one of the swans as her deceased husband Peter. She was relieved by what Peter had come to tell her.

You're crazy. Look around, this is great. Why wouldn't I want to be here. See what I can do.

Samantha describes Peter enthusiastically floating and whizzing around freely. Although he tells her that she is not allowed to see everything he sees, he escorts her to a different scene.

Samantha finds herself resting comfortably on a soft, old fashioned canopied bed. She hears them say that they want her to rest. She has entered a space of healing and release. She pleads.

What did I do wrong, what did I do wrong?

She notices several beings curiously watching and taking notes. They are making a list.

I am the only one who thinks that I did something wrong. The transcriber is saying, okay, now I am going to throw the note away. Watch me. There. Done.

Samantha observes the note being thrown away and disappearing.

OHHHH, now I feel like I can breathe again. I am not in the bed anymore. I am floating again in nothingness. I feel peaceful.

Samantha senses a transition after hearing someone say that she needs a rest. She hears someone talking about her.

Let's send her to a good life.

Once again, the scene shifts. Samantha sees herself in an earlier lifetime. She is a little girl in a white party dress with black patent leather shoes.

Today is my 5th birthday party. There's lots of people here at the party. We are having pony rides. My house is a big house—a plantation. I am running around looking at stuff.

After enjoying the celebration for a few minutes, I suggested that she move ahead to the next most important scene in her life.

I am 18 years old, my name is Olivia. I am at church. I am marrying Sean. I think I wanted this. It's a good thing. I have known him for a while, we grew up together. I am very happy. Sean is equally happy. This is good, all good.

Samantha spontaneously moves to a future scene.

It's a sad moment. Something happened to the baby. The baby died, and I am not doing too well. I am in a bed or a hospital. People are crying. There is no baby… I did something wrong, and that's why the baby died. I am saying I'm sorry, I'm sorry over and over again.

Watching this I know I didn't do anything wrong, but when I view this from Olivia's perspective, she believes she did. She is blaming herself for doing something wrong.

Watching Olivia's experience from the vantage point of the higher soul-self, Samantha experiences compassion for her earlier self.

This poor girl is full of guilt. She continually cries out, what did I do wrong? Even though people are telling her that she didn't do anything wrong, she doesn't believe them. She is crying uncontrollably. No one can console her.

Olivia is overcome with guilt. The baby died when Olivia accidentally rolled over and suffocated her on the bed.

Healing beings are trying to help Samantha wade through her emotions to see the situation from the baby's perspective.

Yes, I can see now that the baby didn't intend to stay alive. Her death was part of her plan. But why would the baby have chosen for me to cause her death?

Samantha is asked whether she can understand that even when the outer world is horrific, things happen according to plan. She again hears the earlier message from the swans and wonders if this is the lesson of both lives.

You did the best you could. Love, love, love.

Olivia struggles with survivor's guilt. She is stuck in a deep, dark depression. She is overburdened by guilt. Unable to carry the burden any longer, she takes an overdose and slips away. As she lifts out of her body, the sadness that she carried for years is released.

Her higher self is surrounded by a bevy of higher beings who have come to help Olivia sort through the sadness and guilt of the loss of her baby. One and the same soul, they are simultaneously providing an opportunity for Samantha to heal the loss of her beloved Peter.

Their words are freeing.

People die. People are born, people die. Regardless of how they die, there is nothing that you can do. You did the best you could. You always do.

Trying to assuage the guilt and remorse, the healing beings are quite repetitive.

> *What are you going to do? people die. Death is out of your control. There is nothing you can or could do. What happened, happened! Death is a part of a higher plan. You are not the architect of those plans.*

Understandably, death can leave people perplexed, sad, hurting, and erroneously feeling guilty or responsible. The higher beings offer Samantha a healing session so that she can anchor the realization that she is not responsible for another's death. They are emphatic in their emphasis that death is a part of the unfolding of a divine plan.

In her earlier life as Olivia, she took her own life, seeing that as the only way to end the pain. In this life as Samantha, she would know that there were other choices.

> *They are offering me encouragement. They are telling me, that I am not bad.*
>
> *You're pretty dam good. So, go live the rest of your life. It is going to be a long one. There is much more to do, more people to love and more people who will love you. Live life fully.*

Despite her experience, Samantha had doubts about the story of her past life as Olivia. Yet she was emphatic that the emotions she experienced and the beliefs held by Olivia were very real and very relevant. She had been shown how the guilt she has been carrying for Peter's death was misdirected and unnecessary and how to release it.

Perhaps the best affirmation that a session has value is the client's words upon awakening. It was clear from Samantha's reaction that her choice of regression therapy was helpful.

> *How interesting, that was the message that I needed to hear. They gave me what I needed. Some sense that there is something beyond this life.*

Losing a loved one is a natural and unavoidable part of life. Your reaction to the loss may signal the need for healing unresolved trauma or reconciling falsely held beliefs from your earlier lives. It may also be your soul's attempt to jar recognition that everyone has their own destiny and the harsh fact of life that ultimately; you have no choice but to accept it.

* * *

In the next case, we meet Julie, who is coping with the greatest loss most can imagine, the death of her child. Her experience shows us how limited life can be when we overreact to the death of loved ones or the circumstances of our own death in prior lives. In the loss of love, there is much to learn.

JULIE

Julie is a 65-year-old retiree. She remains grief stricken a year following the death of her son who struggled with drug and alcohol addiction. She lives alone, having divorced decades before.

For many, the chance to connect to your eternal nature offers comfort that seems nowhere to be found. For Julie, her session offered a chance to do just that. In the process, she was freed from unresolved trauma and given the chance to modify beliefs that had shaped limiting choices.

Once in trance, she finds herself in a life several hundred years ago. She lives a simple, peaceful life in a small cottage in the forest. She has lived alone since the death of her husband. They chose not to have children. She is a natural healer who is highly sought after for the effectiveness of the herbal remedies that she makes.

She spends little time revisiting the details of the life before finding herself floating out of her body after her death. She has lived a very long life. From the perspective of her higher self, whose eternal name is Oriana, we learn the following.

> *I didn't acknowledge the depth of my knowing and spirituality.*
>
> *I had a peaceful life. I was always alone. I liked it. I was just as happy without my husband as I was when he was alive. My freedom was so important. I was free to enjoy all the aspects of nature, the trees and plants, the animals.*

From this higher perspective, we learn about her efforts to achieve balance.

In this past lifetime as a healer, I planned to live a long time to counterbalance a lifetime when I was sacrificed in ancient Egypt.

As a young girl, I was selected to be buried alive with the pharaoh. It was an honor for my family that I was chosen because of my beauty and purity. Honor was everything, life was all about honor.

How twisted and out of balance the pursuit of honor can be to send innocent children to their death.

I really felt cheated in that life. It was not my choice. I had no say, no control. It was not fair, nor was it right. It was my life, not theirs! As a young girl, honor was not important to me. I went along with their decision because it was my duty to do so.

I felt powerless.

I promised myself that in the future I would live a long life to balance the fact that my life was cut so short. I vowed that I would live with the freedom to be myself. I vowed to not be controlled.

And so, after that, I've spent many lives alone to insure my freedom. But I can also see now that I spent too many lifetimes alone.

I can see now that at one level, the young girl made the choice to acquiesce. She neither fought nor ran away. Rather, bound by a strong sense of duty, she accepted her fate. Balancing freedom requires balancing one's sense of duty and obligation.

As the session continued, Julie's higher self elaborated on the importance of freedom in successive life plans, including in her current incarnation. She incorporated freedom into her lives: freedom to choose, freedom to be, and freedom to come and go without restraint. From her higher perspective, she acknowledged the back and forth to achieve the balance that she knows she must strike.

It's a pendulum, it swings one way and then must swing in the other direction. You take one thing to the extreme because of something else. You need to reach a happy medium. It takes careful calibration.

Oriana brings clearer focus to the struggles she is having in her life as Julie.

> *Julie is confused and lost at times. She has done the best she can. On the one hand, she revels in the freedom that she has. But this has kept her busy and distracted. It's preventing her from connecting spiritually. To do so, she must slow down. She needs more quiet time, and she needs to meditate more.*
>
> *The loss of Julie's son brought her to a halt. It stopped her in her tracks.*
>
> *Throughout her career, she was the queen bee, running around helping people. She loved having the freedom to do what she liked. She loved it all, training, teaching, and guiding. Unfortunately, it robbed her of the time she needed to go inward so that she might grow spiritually.*
>
> *Her enthusiastic quest for freedom has pushed her to an extreme. She needs to reach a balance point, to bring the pendulum back to a middle ground. It doesn't have to be all or nothing.*
>
> *She has been hiding away. She needs to not be afraid to love or to get hurt. She needs not to be afraid of the heart. The heart can heal, it can survive. She doesn't have to protect it. The heart always heals. She should not be afraid. She needs to allow herself to be vulnerable.*

These words will resonate for a long time.

When you choose to incarnate on earth, you are given a chance to apply astral lessons. Julie's soul has known for some time that balance was something that she must master, and so she incorporated this challenge into her life plan.

In her regression, Julie was shown how the trauma of her own death several thousand years ago led to many lifetimes in which freedom was out of balance. To protect from future vulnerability, her soul crafted successive life plans centered around freedom, freedom to be, to love, to grow and mature. But in her own words, the pendulum swung too far.

In her current lifetime, she has relished this freedom. It set the stage for her very busy and rewarding lifestyle, until her world came crashing down following the death of her son.

Grief jolted her from the pattern that had worked for so long. Her son's death rendered her coping behaviors ineffective.

In the healing offered by the higher beings, Julie's soul was unburdened. From the safety of their energetic embrace, she was released from her own tight grip of protection. She came to understand that true safety and peace can only be found within, beyond the distractions of daily life.

> *When I was younger, I reveled in the stillness. The colors of the rainbow would wash over me, as they did at the beginning of my regression. This experience reminded me of the serenity I so easily reached when I was younger. I have been reminded how wonderful it feels when there is no place you need to go, nothing you need to do, and nothing you need or want. Just 'being' is enough. Now that I know why I am always running; I can stop long enough to go inward and revel in the silence.*

In soul state, our eternal nature is not only understood, but it is experienced. The unconditional love and acceptance that Julie received from the healing beings during her regression left no doubt of life without end. In it, she can find the peace that she longs for and joy in the anticipation of someday being reunited with her son. It was also a powerful reminder that shattered any illusion that death is final.

In the counseling session that followed, Julie remarked that she had been freed to choose what she will do in the future. In the immediate, she was certain.

> *I want to help to create a heaven on earth.*

How you died in prior lives can distort beliefs, which in turn leads you to overcompensate. The pain that Oriana's soul carried through time shaped choices that were limiting. By choosing freedom to protect herself, she lost out on the spiritual growth that comes when we open ourselves to love others. It took the death of her son for her to see that she has to break the pattern of isolation that has insulated her from loss and the rich exchange of love that can be found through relationships with others.

* * *

In the next section we are introduced to Dorothea. Like Oriana, protecting herself from the searing pain of lost love had become a driving force in many lives, including her current one.

Dorothea

Dorothea is 43 years old and single, having had one long-term relationship that ended a decade before. During a guided imagery, her beloved grandmother had appeared and urged her to thaw her *frozen heart.* Her decision to do so was the main reason for pursuing regression therapy.

Over the course of several counseling and regression sessions, additional background information would come to light that was critical to better understanding Dorothea's frozen heart. As often happens, when people seek regression therapy, some problems have layers of entanglements that begin to loosen.

Dorothea grew up in a family impacted by her father's alcoholism. Still in elementary school, she saw her father sexually abuse her sister, and turned to other adults in the family to put a stop to it. A series of events cascaded out of control, resulting in her father's accidental overdose and Dorothea being scapegoated by some family members for the crisis. The fallout led her, at age twelve, to consider taking her own life. Fortunately, she didn't.

Several years later, Dorothea met and fell in love with Christian. As first loves can be, Dorothea was overjoyed by the excitement and magic. For a time, the emotional tumult of the past seemed to evaporate. But her fairy-tale romance would come crashing down when she discovered that she was just one of Christian's many loves. Her anger soon dissolved into depression, one that led her once again to contemplate suicide to put a stop to the pain. For a second time, she chose life.

Fifteen years passed, with only a handful of casual first dates, before Dorothea met Marcus and began an eight-year long relationship. Throughout the course of their relationship, she had no desire to marry. In the last year they were together, her sentiments shifted. But Marcus had no interest in a long-term committed relationship. For several years after their breakup, she shielded herself from all possibility of dating. Her grandmother's telepathic message during a guided imagery nudged the issue front and center.

During her third regression, Dorothea revisited a lifetime in the 1920s in which she lived on a vineyard with her husband Mario. Her name was

Bethany. After several years, she became pregnant. Sickened by blood poisoning, she lost the baby and almost died herself. Following the ordeal, she and her husband were devastated as their dream to start a family had been shattered. He feared for her life, while she blamed herself for the loss of the baby. Subsequent attempts to give birth ended in multiple miscarriages, which just deepened her despair.

With no clear understanding of the workings of depression and desperate to make her happy again, Mario adopted a baby without consulting with her. Although Mario brought home the *gift* he thought she would want, his gesture of love had the opposite effect. Bethany began to drink, worsening her overall condition. Having fallen deeper into despair, five years after the miscarriage, she attempted to end her life. Once again, Mario brought her back from the brink.

Connecting to Bethany's pain, Dorothea's heart aches with the vivid recall of the power of Mario's love. She is overcome with emotion. In her recollections, she sees that she stood ready to jump to her death as Mario pleaded for her life.

> *Mario is begging me to stay, he's telling me how important I am in his life and that he doesn't want to live life without me. He loves me and needs me. He is telling me to be strong and courageous; and that our love for each other is enough. There is always hope.*
>
> *I was hanging on by a thread.*
>
> *After the miscarriage, I was very depressed. I didn't leave the house. I was suicidal. I was in so much pain, physically and emotionally, that it was easier at times to think about just giving-up to stop the suffering.*
>
> *His love convinced me to stay.*

Mario's love instilled a sense of hope that would not be realized as Bethany's drinking worsened.

Several years later, they agreed to foster two young relatives whose parents were unable to care for them. Bethany learned to appreciate the fact that she had raised several children who loved her. But although she loved them, this would never fill the gaping hole in her heart.

For the remainder of her life, she would struggle with depression as well as alcohol addiction. She would die holding a false belief that *love and pain were one and the same.*

On her last day of her life, Bethany, now 70, was out for a walk when she collapsed and died. Seeing herself float out of her body, she's surprised that she's dead. She laughs at the irony that it happened so fast, reflecting back to her prior suicidal thoughts and thwarted attempts to kill herself, the first time after the first miscarriage and the second time after Mario died twenty years before.

Bethany finds herself surrounded by a cadre of higher beings. The soul of Mario joins her. As their hearts connect, she realizes that he is Marcus, her lover earlier in her current life as Dorothea. The pair are enveloped in the loving embrace of the higher beings. She later remarked.

I saw my heart. It was encased in ice. I saw that it began to melt.

She recalls that with Mario's love, she had plowed through despair and chosen life. She did so with the painful understanding that loss accompanies both love and life.

Bethany reflects on her life, one that knew the joy of love and the pain of love. She is reminded that life and love can die, but that both are eternal. She is helped to understand that the beauty and joy that is given freely within a loving relationship are the most valuable gifts humans exchange.

She is bathed in the loving energy of the Source God and is surrounded by a light that grows brighter and warmer. In the relief, she is unburdened of the sadness of the past and freed to find and revel in love.

In the first of a number of counseling sessions that followed, Dorothea spoke of the direct connection between Bethany's tragic life and her earlier decisions to never marry and to not have children.

She admitted that, after her break-up with Christian decades before, she vowed that she would be guarded for the rest of her life. This was a promise to herself that she kept even during her relationship with Marcus. In the regression, she was stirred by the visceral experience of seeing her frozen heart begin to melt as she embraced her beloved Mario. She knew at that moment that her prior determination to remain guarded had been weakened. The ice had begun to thaw.

Twice before reaching the age of twenty, Dorothea had contemplated suicide to ease the pain of the betrayal of trust by her father, family members, and her first love. Bethany had needed the strength of others not to end her life. But a century later, Dorothea would prove to herself that she had the strength and courage to survive. When she chose life, she rewrote a belief formed years before, that love and pain are one and the same.

Within months of this dramatic session, Dorothea began dating, and laughingly announced that she'd begun the search for the man of her dreams. In her words:

I have taken my first steps off the carousel of despair.

* * *

Shattered dreams too often lead to future decisions based on a belief that loving isn't worth the risk. Like Dorothea, the client we meet in the next section came to equate love with loss, erecting a barrier that would shield her from that possibility.

Ashley

Ashley is a 30-year-old yoga instructor who agreed to the request of her anxious friend to accompany her to a past life regression. And then she decided, based on her friend's coaxing, to schedule her own session. She didn't believe that she could be hypnotized and approached the session with skepticism.

Initially challenged to remain at the trance depth she achieved, I coaxed her into a relaxed state. I then suggested that she imagine that she was writing a novel and asked her to select the type of novel, setting, time frame, and protagonist in her story.

For her story, she chose a romantic novel set in England. Her main character is 25-year-old Helen who meets the love of her life while at the local market.

Her novel opens.

One day I noticed him shopping for groceries. I was intrigued. There seems to be an instantaneous connection. We see each other at the store for a few weeks before we speak. I decided to take the initiative.

I pretend to drop my bag of groceries so that he will help me pick them up. The fruit splatters. We are both laughing. He finally asks me my name. His name is David. It seems that he was simply waiting for the right moment to finally introduce himself and ask me out to dinner.

By the time Ashley reaches this point in her story, it is clear that she has slipped into a deeper trance and is relaying the events of a past life.

We are at an Italian restaurant having pizza. It so easy to talk to him. We make plans to see each other again. Afterward, he walks me home. As we say goodnight, we kiss.

Helen moves ahead in time.

We are at the park, having a picnic. David's dog Buddy is with us. We have been dating over the last three months. We are so happy and comfortable together. We are falling in love and have been talking about moving in together. I want to move out of my parent's house. He has an apartment. So, I will move in with him.

Prompted to move ahead to the next most significant time, we arrive at Helen and David's wedding.

We are in a small church. It is filled with beautiful pink roses that smell so beautiful. I am wearing a long dress with lacy sleeves. My veil covers my light brown hair which is pulled up. David is wearing a bow tie with his black suit. We are saying our vows in the presence of our families and friends.

At the next prompting, Helen moves ahead two years. She has just given birth to their first child and is holding her new baby boy.

His name is Michael. I am in the hospital. Our parents and friends are here with us. David is deliriously happy, but he is also nervous. He feels unprepared. We knew that we wanted a baby, but we didn't plan for it to be so soon. David's apartment is big enough for us now, but we are thinking about having more kids so we will need to make a change. We are planning to move outside of London to a more rural area. It will be a challenge leaving the excitement of the city, especially the parks and pubs.

Once again, Helen moves ahead another several years. It's her daughter Cindy's second birthday. The family has moved outside the city and cherishes their outside yard. Helen has put her career as a teacher on hold and stays home to take to take care of the children. David is still working long hours in the city in an advertising agency.

We are happy with the kids. But we don't get enough sleep, so we are often tired. We argue about little things because we are both so irritable. Because of David's hours and long commute, I pretty much take care of the children myself. It's quite demanding, so I don't have much time to spend with my friends or by myself. We have decided not to have any more children.

Five years later, Helen sees that with David's backing she has returned to teaching. Both of their parents are pitching in to make the new arrangement work. David's support has brought them closer together, and life together is filled with the happiness that they both hoped and planned.

Helen moves ahead again. She is attending David's funeral. His death from cancer was fast and unexpected. She sees herself and the children, who are now in their 20s. Crying, she is overcome with emotion. Her voice breaks.

I feel so alone. I don't know what I will do without him. It's scary to think about being alone for the rest of my life. I have been trying to hold it in for the children and the others.

Helen sees herself at home a year after the funeral.

I have mostly been going through the motions of life this past year. My grief turned to anger at the world. It wasn't fair. I was robbed of David. I took my anger out on people who weren't to blame. Now I am alone and isolated. I know that I have to move on. I dream about traveling someday.

Seven years after losing her beloved David, Helen sees herself traveling through Indonesia on what she labels an open-ended adventure. She was drawn to the nation's archipelago of more than a thousand islands because it was not like any place she had been before. Despite the adventure and the beauty, she is still saddened by the loss of her partner, her best friend.

I miss David so much. I don't think I can ever love someone in the same way. I sense David's presence even in my dreams. It feels like he is still with me in many ways.

Decades pass, and Helen finds herself in a hospital back home in England. She has spent the years alone reticent to risk loving again. She has been sick for about a year with an unspecified illness. Despite that, she has just celebrated her eightieth birthday.

As she sees herself float out of her body after she dies, she notes how light and unburdened she feels. We are now hearing from the perspective of her eternal soul-self.

When I look back at this life, I can see that it was filled with love, family, and adventure. I do have some regrets.

I so wish that David had lived longer. We could have shared all those adventures.

I was so lonely, all those years spent alone. The travel was an escape. It was too difficult to remain in the home that we had created together, where we started our family. I had to make a change. I could no longer live that life without him. That's why I went to Indonesia. It was not only exotic—it was very, very far away.

I ran away but I could not start all over. I was afraid to love again.

In this space beyond time, Helen is gifted with an energetic healing. She is encouraged to let go of any fears or reservations that remain. The higher beings want her to discharge any reluctance that she may be holding onto. They are freeing residue from the past.

Helen is encouraged to remember the depth of her love for David, to feel it and to allow it to radiate out. She imagines a starburst emanating from her heart as she affirms that loving David was worth the risk of losing him.

In the space beyond time, she holds the understanding of love unlimited, love unhindered. She feels the infusion of energy and vitality from the higher beings filling every space and crevice in her being.

Remembering the beauty of the love she shared with David, she says.

> *In future lives, I won't be afraid to fall in love again. I need to remember not to hide from the joy that love has to offer.*

In the follow-up discussion, Ashley acknowledged that the experience was both real and relevant.

> *Pretty early in the story, I experienced a shift from making it up to reliving it. It was my story. It makes sense. I never have had a serious relationship. Although I haven't ever thought of myself as holding back, I can relate to having a subconscious fear that I need to avoid being hurt.*

Ashley added that she could feel Helen's sadness and loneliness as a tightness in her stomach. She recalled the same feeling when meeting someone and worrying that she might be swept off her feet.

> *Then you get a knot in your stomach and say to yourself 'boy, I better get out of this before there is no turning back.'*

Despite the surface circumstances that brought Ashley to have a past life regression, it was clear that her guides had been involved in orchestrating the session. They wanted to remind her of the promise she had made to herself to not hide from the joy that love has to offer. They didn't want her to let the possibility of losing love, stop her from loving.

They were heartened that she got the message as she acknowledged, *that's good advice.*

Building a wall to protect yourself is a natural and understandable reaction to a broken heart. Some people spend years, or lifetimes, keeping an emotional distance because they believe it is too dangerous to love.

But as Helen's life shows us, what is lost is too often a heavy price to pay. Ultimately, love is worth the risk of losing it. Or, as has been said by many guides:

The experience of love, although painful, gives meaning to life.

Perhaps you too have lost someone you dearly loved. If so, you know the searing pain that feels as if it will never go away.

I have heard it said most clearly from one client whose heart was broken when his first love decided to end their relationship. He described being devasted and surprised at how long it took to regain any sense of future direction and interest in life.

Our use of the term broken heart is an apt description. Before it mends, we lose our desire to connect to others. We remain unable or unwilling to allow ourselves to care and engage more than superficially with others. Our bodies seem capable of robotically going through the day-to-day motions while we remain numb and often disconnected from life. I liken it to pressing a giant pause button.

A harsh truth that most learn to accept in life is that not everyone who loves us, or professes never ending love, will be able to honor their words. Many circumstances contribute, death being the most obvious, but there are others.

All of us can benefit from learning to look beyond loss to answer a key question. What does our soul yearn for us to discover through the loss? An answer awaits. If there is a pattern of loss that recurs, it may be a clue that we have yet to dive deep to uncover the lesson that longs for discovery.

I had a client whose personal and professional life dramatically illustrates this point. Both were filled with unimaginable losses. He lost both parents, two siblings, his first wife, and two of his closest friends, all before he reached 28. He is a renowned surgeon who specialized in treating people with brain cancer. And although he has successfully treated many hundreds of patients, many of the people referred to him did not survive.

He chose past life regression to gain some understanding of what was behind all the losses.

In his regression, he visited several lives, each with trauma leading to unbearable loss. In multiple lives, he was the only survivor, left with survivor's guilt. These lives reinforced a belief that life was so filled with suffering that it wasn't worth living; a belief that the soul cannot leave unbalanced.

Eventually, his soul decided to move to resolution, planning to create in his current life the circumstances that would surface the unbalanced belief with the intent of bringing it into balance. Unlike in the prior lives, in which he succumbed to the losses, this life's spotlight on the issue prompted healing. With each successive loss, he now finds himself more deeply appreciative of the beauty and joy that life holds. His attitudinal buoyancy on the issue is strengthened through his surviving patients.

His capacity to love, despite the countless losses, has deepened.

What do you really believe about love and the risk of losing it? Your answer may be a clue to what happened in the past and how it is shaping your future. Perhaps you have never understood why you seem to hold conflicting views about relationships. And maybe, like Dorothea, Julie, Ashley, Freja, and Samantha, you need to be freed from unresolved trauma and helped to release beliefs that are robbing you of deep and satisfying connections.

Forgiveness is giving up the hope that the past could have been any different, it's accepting the past for what it was, and using this moment and this time to help yourself move forward.

—OPRAH WINFREY

4

Forgiveness

You may have heard the above quote, and if you have been working to forgive yourself or someone else, you may agree.

What can't be forgiven weighs us down. In fact, if you carry the emotional burden of the actions of someone else, who may have long ago forgotten their transgression or never realized their wrongdoing in the first place, you are the one who is suffering. Choosing to stew in anger over a wrongdoing, or projecting blame, will become intractable at some future time.

Your other choice is to forgive, and through the forgiveness; to move on, free of the burden of the impact of someone else's mistake. In choosing forgiveness, you are deciding to no longer give someone rent free space in your mind and heart.

Once you accept your own divine essence, you must also accept that everyone else is a divine being, even when they act like they have forgotten long ago. This is an extremely difficult challenge when the one needing forgiveness has done unspeakable or egregious things.

Remembering that earth is a school is important. Accepting that all of us who remain in the earth school have more things to learn makes it easier to accept the fact that, until we graduate, all of us are still making mistakes.

Forgiving provides relief. And understanding what your soul planned to gain through the experience offers additional growth. Actively working to forgive helps to highlight long held beliefs and the coping behaviors that have been shaped by them.

*   *   *

In the cases that follow, we will see how the process of uncovering beliefs and associated feelings and behaviors led each of these clients to forgive themselves and others. In so doing, they have accomplished what their soul planned for this lifetime, freedom to revel in their divine essence.

PATRICIA

Patricia is a 32-year-old nurse practitioner with a doctoral degree. Despite her advanced education, she is finding herself pulled in a different career direction. She feels that the risk of making a mistake looms large and believes that something is holding her back from realizing her full potential. She scheduled a session hoping to gain understanding of the origin of the beliefs that are holding her back, with the intent of removing them.

In trance, she finds herself as a 30-year-old male named Daniel who is imprisoned. It is 1783, during peace time in the United States. Dressed in a military uniform, he is unaware what led to his incarceration. Although no war rages, he feels as if he is still fighting the War of Independence. His confusion and anxiety are palpable.

As the next scene unfolds, Daniel sees himself with his head down, standing with his hands on a chair at a large table. He is at the home of someone in the command.

> *I'm carrying the weight of something that has happened.*
>
> *There's a secret, and I have part of it. I heard one of the men in the company blurt out the information. I am confused about how I ended up imprisoned, I don't know what happened. I am waiting for someone to tell me what my fate will be.*

Daniel moves ahead in time.

I must leave the colonies and return home to England. I did something wrong and have been found guilty. I shared a secret with someone I thought I could trust. He is another soldier.

Reflecting some degree of denial, Daniel cannot remember the secret that he revealed. He does recall that, as a result, a strategic maneuver during the war had to be aborted.

I buried it. I don't think anyone died.

I didn't realize that by sharing the secret with the other soldier that it might change the outcome of a battle.

Going back will be a different kind of jail. It will be a jail of my own making.

Daniel acknowledges that his mistake was inadvertent but will not let himself off the hook.

I will punish myself.

I should have known better than to trust the man. I had reservations about the man, but I ignored them. My gut told me not to trust him, but I did because of fear. I was afraid of not seeming strong, of being a fool. I wanted to act like I knew more, that I have it all together. But the man poked at my pride, so I told him. And now, I have all this guilt.

Now I will live in a prison of shame.

Moving ahead in time, Daniel finds himself standing on a dock. He has just arrived back home in England. He is gazing out across the water toward America.

I am very angry. I am angry at everyone, including myself. I will hide. No one must know that I am here. The war was lost by England, and I am lost with it.

It seems, although Daniel was British, he had chosen to move to the colonies and then patriotically served with colonial forces. Despite his part in the secret being revealed, the colonial forces prevailed. Banishing him back to his motherland, which had been defeated by the colonial forces, was indeed a harsh punishment. Even before he reached the motherland, his debacle was in the newspapers.

Everyone knows. There is so much shame.

My family lives here. They once were important. My family's status has already declined. My family is worried about the future. They wonder how I will marry.

I have not been disavowed. But I am isolating myself because of my shame. I am very much alone. I am worried that people will not understand and that I will be ostracized.

Once again, Daniel moves ahead in time. He finds himself in his family's home, sitting in front of the fire. It's Christmas. The atmosphere is relaxed and comfortable. Everyone is acting like old times. They have welcomed him back.

I'm broke. I am very sad. Everyone's trying to lift me up, but I am not allowing them to do it.

There is no pressure from my family, they just want me back. But we have no money. Although I am comfortable sitting here, I am wondering how do I support myself and the family? My role is to take care of them. My father is old, I am the only male.

Daniel moves to his last day in life. He is 83, sick in bed. To support the family, he found work as a scribe. He sees himself gently slip away and float out of his body. Once in soul state, he is able to reflect back on his entire life. Despite many decades since his earlier debacle, he has yet to forgive himself.

At big important moments involving a big decision, I failed myself. I ignored my intuition. At important junctures, I can't trust myself. If I made the wrong choice, how do I trust myself?

The soul self of Daniel is joined by a cadre of higher beings capable of facilitating release and healing. He is quiet as they work to help him move beyond the burden his soul has carried for too long.

Several minutes later, the soul self indicates that it is able to forgive the mistake made in Daniel's life and that it is time to free Patricia from carrying the burden of past errors in judgement.

> *It was just a mistake. I was only human. It is time to learn to trust my intuition and strengthen my capacity for discernment. Despite having some reservations about this, I am ready to move ahead.*
>
> *It's time to free myself from the prison of my own making. It's time for Patricia to live life to her fullest potential. It is something that was denied Daniel, but that I can gift Patricia. Through this, my soul goes forward, free of the regret.*

Brought to a place of freedom and forgiveness, Daniel's soul basks in self-acceptance. Feeling the power of the freedom and forgiveness, he allows the light of his divinity to shine brightly. He knows deep in his being that he is on a journey to allow his divine perfection to unfold.

Up from trance, Patricia is excited to tell me of what she saw when the higher beings joined her.

> *I saw the face of an angel in my third eye. Then my life started going in rewind as the angel appeared. I rewound to the moment when I let the other soldier trick me. I replayed that moment and didn't let him do that.*
>
> *I didn't even tell you before we began that I have trouble trusting my intuition. I couldn't get past the blockage to trust it, even though I received many signs.*

Daniel's experience crystalized doubt. The doubt carried into Patricia's life and overrode her intuition. No matter how strong her intuition became, doubt prevailed. This contributed to the very problem that brought her to schedule her regression session. Indecision leading to inaction. In common terms; she was stuck.

With the understanding she gained, she was able to unravel falsely held beliefs that were eroding her self-confidence and formulate more accurate beliefs. Holding new, balanced beliefs about her own intuitive capacities, she has a clearer sense of the real risks involved in shifting career focus.

Patricia's higher self found forgiveness in the healing release that she experienced. Unburdened from this weight, she ceased recriminations over a bad decision that was made more than two centuries ago. Forgiving herself became the first step to trusting herself, allowing her to move forward with the important decisions and exciting choices that lay ahead.

A year after her session, Patricia excitedly told me that she started a new business, building on the training and skills that she had developed originally as a hobby. The new direction is a perfect match for her talents, as well as the work that makes her heart sing.

* * *

In the next case, we are introduced to Art. Like Patricia, events that unfolded hundreds of years before left emotional scars and created false beliefs that have been brought forward by his soul into his current life for healing and resolution. Art suffered greatly due to the malicious actions of others. His path to forgiveness for the actions of others in his current life winds through understanding and resolution of past transgressions by others.

Art

Art is a 60-year-old chemist who scheduled a regression to explore how past life experiences are affecting his current lifetime.

In discussions prior to trance, he mentioned three situations reflecting themes of powerlessness and forgiveness. His intuition would prove correct, as the themes played out in his visit to an earlier lifetime.

Art is working to forgive his mother for emotionally abandoning him. A recent family drama prompted her to confess a long-held secret that she had hoped to never reveal. She had given her first child up for adoption. It led to heart wrenching discussions in which she acknowledged that Art bore the brunt of her lifelong unhappiness. Her apology for years of emotional neglect and abuse had yet to give him the inner peace that he desires.

More recently, a co-worker spread a bizarre falsity that threatened his decades-long tenure in a major pharmaceutical firm when he was within reach of retirement.

Initially, I felt helpless and powerless, as I did with my mother. But I knew I had to stand-up for myself. I fought them and won.

Lastly, decades ago, his first love became pregnant. Their different religious backgrounds precluded marriage and led them to decide to abort. He shared:

I have never forgiven myself.

Art mentioned that he had a prior session with a psychic who referenced several prior lifetimes, leaving him wondering about the crossover in his current life. In one life, he was a woman in China in the early 1900s. She had organized a network of people to help women who could not keep their babies. Her group smuggled the babies out of the country after finding families that wanted to adopt them. In a second life, he was a medical doctor living on the Canadian frontier in the 1800s who helped women who worked in a brothel stay healthy and avoid pregnancy. And in a third life, he was a slave girl forced to be a concubine.

It was this latter life that he would revisit in trance. The slave girl was named Maura.

I am 20 years old and have been in the harem for four years. There is no good way to survive. My family only endured life's many hardships. Being a concubine was considered a good life. Agreeing to become one however has not turned out as I hoped.

I am beautiful, with brown eyes and have curly dark hair. It was considered an honor to be selected.

There are 20 of us. I was one of the master's favorites. Jealousy is common. I am isolated and have no friends.

Even though there was mutual love and tenderness between us, he shares me with his associates. This makes me feel worthless. I believe I gave him my heart.

Maura moves ahead in time and finds herself in an alley screaming in pain, ignored by passers-by.

I have been kicked out of the harem by the master and am not sure what to do. I was pregnant with his child. But I was falsely accused. One of the other slave girls rumored that I had prostituted myself and that the baby was fathered by one of the master's rivals. The master was jealous of this rival, so he believed the rumor.

I was well along in the pregnancy but was banished from the palace. I don't feel good about this. I am not well. I started early labor and headed into an alley. I'm crying and feeling hopeless. I am calling out to those who are passing, but no one is coming to help.

My screams are ignored.

With no preparation for what to expect, Maura gives birth to a baby boy.

The baby is screaming. I don't know how to handle this. There is something wrong with the umbilical cord. I don't know what to do. I am in pain. The baby slips away in my arms.

I want to die too. There's nothing to live for. So, I think I will kill myself.

Floating out of her body and into soul state, Maura is now free of the physical and emotional pain of her short life. In the presence of higher beings, she reflects back.

Although there wasn't a practical or easy way to stand-up for myself, I am blaming myself for not doing so. I blame myself for the baby's death. I didn't know how to care for him.

In future lives, I need to be careful about having sex. I know there must be a better way to survive and take care of one's self than as a courtesan. Love leads to anguish. I am not sure how I feel about being vulnerable in the future. Love hardens the heart.

I wonder why the master didn't take my word? Instead, he believed the rumors rather than me. Why didn't he trust me? I had been faithful.

I blame myself for getting pregnant. I made a mistake. I wanted to be closer to the master. It would have solidified my position with him.

Having revisited his life as Maura, Art uncovers the betrayal that led to Maura's death. From this perspective, his higher self sees how distorted both the experience of love and compassion were. Maura's love was not reciprocated. Betrayed, she was shown no compassion by her lover or the strangers who saw her suffer in the street. The trauma created an imbalance that ricocheted across two millennia. And, in this lifetime, has limited his capacity to forgive.

The higher beings counsel Art on how to move forward to heal the sorrow.

You've demonstrated love and compassion in your subsequent lives, caring for the women in the brothel and finding adoptive homes. But there were another twenty lifetimes in which compassion has not been balanced. You are close to bringing it into balance in this life.

You should live with compassion for everyone, no matter who they are. Love everyone.

As he revisited Maura's life, Art realized that the woman who spread the false rumors about the pregnancy is his mother in his current life. This explains the depth of his lifelong struggle to forgive her for emotional abuse and neglect. The task of forgiving her has increased exponentially.

We encourage you to have love, forgiveness, and compassion for your mother.

Art is being shown how forgiving her for her mistakes in this and the earlier life is an important part of unburdening his heart. The capacity for forgiveness can be found through compassion for himself and the others who have harmed him in this life and previous ones.

The higher beings selected Art's life as a concubine to revisit instead of the other 19 in which compassion was a challenge. Their selection was quite purposeful, as Maura's life included lessons about powerlessness.

The decision that Maura made to allow herself to get pregnant was motivated in part by her natural desire to be loved and solidify the master's love. But her decision not to stand-up for herself sealed her fate and the fate of her baby. This caused her to falsely accept responsibility for the baby's death and reinforced her sense of worthlessness.

Like Maura, Art had a natural desire to be loved. But it was his comparable decision not to more assertively stand-up for himself and challenge his mother's long-standing mistreatment that has carried emotional wounds from childhood well into adulthood.

In each of the circumstances, calling out for forgiveness, there was a sub-theme highlighted—no capacity to care for a baby. Perhaps no other type of case tests our capacity for compassion for ourselves and others than those involving the loss through death, abortion, or adoption of child. Characteristic of these cases is the strength that souls exhibit as the dramas surrounding babies and children play out. It is important to remember when considering these that each soul has made and agreed to its own life plan, including lives that are extremely brief. We know from life between lives research that each soul embeds goals in the life plan it makes for the upcoming lifetime. Included among the myriad goals is being of service to another.

As just one example of both these points, consider the soul who is in the midst of planning a lifetime that will not begin for some extended period of time. During the interim, that soul is approached by a member of his soul family who is making a soul plan for her own life to expand her capacity for compassion. To set the circumstances for compassion to develop, she requests that he play a role as her newborn infant who will die within hours of birth. The soul agrees to assume this brief role and puts his own plan on hold temporarily. His brief life will be of service to hers. Once he has finished playing this role, he returns to resume the planning that he had briefly suspended. What plays out as a human tragedy is the agreement of two soul family members supporting each other in their spiritual growth.

In the discussion following the session, Art noted that he experienced a major shift.

He was stunned by the thematic connections between the past lives and his current life, including discovering that four soul family members assumed key roles in both lives.

He acknowledged that the healing that began in the recent months will need to continue, but he could already sense that resolution was within reach. In the past, one minute with his mother would have thrown him back into feeling worthless. But he had come to see that he is not powerless, nor was Maura.

I feel like I am on the right path. It is really amazing and empowering.

In an update, months after his session, Art had made significant progress. He has deepened his forgiveness and compassion for his mother, and in doing so has freed himself from the tight grip that the recent and distant past held over him.

* * *

Next, we will meet Kerry whose strong sense of duty and responsibility have left her unable to see that there was nothing to forgive.

Kerry

Kerry is a 56-year-old married engineer who is within two years of retirement.

Before her hypnotic journey, she described several situations that have defined her relationships within her small nuclear family. While a teen, her mother's controlling behavior stymied her first significant romantic relationship and landed her under psychiatric care. On the advice of her therapist, she moved into the home of family friends who she considers a bonus family.

Kerry views the trauma that resulted from these early years of upheaval as derailing her life. She readily admits that her parents influenced her choice of a safe occupation that has provided little joy over three decades.

Eight years ago, Kerry's parents died within months of each other. Kerry and her sibling became coexecutors of their parents' estate. Her close relationship with her sister, who moved into their parents' home, began to fray over differing views on how to execute the estate. The situation was complicated by the after-effects of a near death accident that left her sister with impaired judgement and unable to work for the last 15 years.

Kerry's hopes to settle the estate and use the proceeds to assure her sister's future financial security were stymied by her sister's procrastination and suspicions that Kerry was out to cheat her.

Her sister has used the drama of Kerry's strained relationship with her parents during her teens and twenties to assert an emotional and financial claim to the estate.

I deserve everything because I loved mom and dad more than you did.

Kerry recently hired a lawyer, unable herself to resolve the stalemate after seven years.

She scheduled her past life session hoping to gain an understanding about these troubling family dynamics.

Sensing that her capacity to live the balance of her life in joy and peace is reliant on her doing so, she hoped that the regression would give her insight that could inform future decisions and heal the rift with her sister.

Kerry's experience is an example of a regression that does not follow linear time. At the outset, she views the life at age 40, then moves back to age 14, then to age 20, then back further to age 7, and then finally to age 78.

Once in trance, Kerry finds herself living as a man of about 40 in a life in the mid-1800s. He is the lord of a manor house who lives with his younger sister. Neither are married. The estate, which has been in the family for centuries, is farmed by a large cadre of staff who address him as Sir James. Unsettled, he sees himself ambling in the library of the manor. He is aware that he is bored, unhappy, and anxious, but is unsure what circumstances precipitated theses emotions.

I move him back through time to determine what has led him to this point in time.

James finds himself at 14, arguing with his father about his future. He loves art and wants to follow his passion as an artist. His father refuses to hear of it, insisting otherwise.

Your art is frivolous and silly. As my only son, you must assume responsibility for this land and home. You are a nobleman.

The manor house and farm have been in James' family for generations. As is customary during the times, he will not only inherit it but be expected to support his parents and young sister Lillie.

James next finds himself in his 20s, away at school. He is at a café with his friends.

I feel free, so thankful to be at school with friends who share my interest in art. There is a woman in the group named Rosalie that I am romantically interested in. Our feelings are reciprocal.

Unfortunately, despite our mutual feelings, at the end of university, I must go back home. Rosalie wants to follow her art and passion. Life at the manor house, in the middle of nowhere, is not what she wants.

Clearly emotional at the memory of lost love and dashed dreams, Kerry is crying as she relays the details of James' decisions.

That was the fork in the road, in which I had a choice to do something different. I didn't take it. I allowed duty to be the dominant variable in my life. I didn't buck the system. I felt a sense of duty and obligation to my family.

I felt resentful, but I also felt like somehow my father would feel guilty making me give up my dreams. But it never really hurt him, it just hurt me.

I felt such a strong sense of duty, I felt I couldn't shirk that duty and responsibility. I guess I always believed that if I fulfilled my obligations, then I would be rewarded with something. I felt the Universe would reward me in some other way because I had to let Rosalie go, that it would be made right.

But sadly, it didn't work out that way.

James moves further back in time. He sees himself at 7-years-old in grade school. He realizes that he had a younger brother Michael. Even at that young age, James hopes that his brother will assume responsibility for the home and farm, freeing James to pursue his interest. But his hopes are dashed as he next recalls that a drowning accident took Michael's life when he was only 10 years old.

The tragedy is made worse by their father's projection of blame for the accident onto James. Although it is unclear whether he had any direct accountability, in a decision that would seal his fate, James accepted the responsibility.

I should have been able to save him. I don't deserve to be happy.

The emotion and memory of the death jolts Kerry back into her own life. She is recalling her sister's near-death accident 25 years ago that spared her life but exerted a great toll. Once again, she is overcome with emotion.

The sister I knew and loved growing up was never the same. Even though she is older by six years, I have been somewhat of a caretaker since then.

Back in trance, a second life as a young woman briefly flashes before her. She is aware that something terrible has happened to a young girl who was in her care. She is distraught and again crying.

With the hope of facilitating a release, I call in the soul of the young girl for an exchange. Kerry expresses her remorse.

I am so sorry. I am just so sorry.

The young girl, who appears fine, replies.

It is okay. There is nothing you could have or should have done that you didn't do. You need to forgive yourself.

Kerry indicates that James' brother Michael is also present and that he has echoed the same sentiments. Despite this, she is not sure initially that she can forgive herself.

I can try.

> *I am more likely to be able to forgive myself now that they have told me that there is nothing more I could have done. It wasn't my fault.*

Kerry's first words after she was brought out of trance suggest that she is ready to integrate the insight she gained.

> *I believe I have the threads of the tapestry. Now it's up to me to decide what to do with it. It's very helpful knowing this.*

She grasps the brilliance of her souls' plan to resurface beliefs and feelings of duty and obligation in her current life for ultimate resolution. The drama of her teenage years left her too ready to appease her parents and pursue their dreams for her lifetime.

> *I had to live the life they wanted me to live because I was still carrying a strong sense of duty and obligation.*

In fact, her more recent exhaustive struggle to ensure the best plan for her sister through settlement of her parents' estate is framed by this very same obligation. It took unjustified accusations by an uncle who decided to weigh in about the estate to finally prompt her to hire a lawyer.

> *I was being treated like a felon that can't be forgiven, as if I should be making restitution.*

Revisiting the lives of James and the young woman surfaced her long-held views of duty and responsibility. Carried into this life, these beliefs shaped feelings and behaviors. Once unraveled, Kerry is free to formulate new beliefs.

Understanding the soul's role in life planning prompts you to ask *what did my soul wish to accomplish by setting the stage for this drama to unfold?* Holding this broader perspective preempts accepting responsibility for outcomes that are not yours.

Those who understand that souls craft plans for upcoming lifetimes can more readily accept the dramas and traumas that occur in life and the lives of others.

Accepting the soul's role in a life plan cut short or filled with suffering requires surrender to divine planning—holding that truth paves the way for forgiveness, forgiveness of self and others. In that knowing surfaces the realization that what happened could not have been any different. This understanding is liberating. It can free you as it's freed Kerry. In her words:

> *I know my next chapter will be more meaningful. Lifting this off of my heart will free me to revel in life's joy and peace!*

* * *

Next, we are introduced to Neil. His regression helps uncover the origin of his self-loathing and the need for him to forgive himself for prior decisions and actions.

NEIL

Neil is a 50-year-old divorcee who has been estranged from his wife and two teenage sons for more than a decade. He is currently employed as a bartender and part time tennis coach. He presents as self-confident, but this veneer falls away as he describes his struggles with alcohol. His past bouts of sobriety have been short lived, although he recently reached six months of abstinence.

He scheduled a regression session with a hope of uncovering the origin of his self-loathing. He feels strongly that there is something below the surface that keeps pulling him down.

Once in trance, Neil finds himself in a life a thousand years ago in the far east. He and his brother are members of the emperor's inner circle of advisors. Despite his royal status, life has been far from joyous in the last few years. There is great strife in the territory controlled by the emperor. Crop failures and no rollback of the taxes have left the populace starving. There are rumblings within the ranks of advisors, fueled by self-interest and self-protection, that culminates in a plan to unseat the emperor. Before it unfolds, loyalists expose the plan. Although Neil is only peripherally involved, he is swept up and arrested, as the coup is being led by his older brother.

Neil begins to sob as he relays the two choices he was given. He was to either kill his brother and be banished from the territory or be killed along with his brother. A torturous decision, he chose to save himself. He is crying hysterically as he describes killing his brother.

I killed him to save myself.

Once exiled, his life became a living hell; his struggle for physical survival punctuated only by the remorse for his betrayal. Unable to overcome the sadness and guilt, he eventually ended his own life.

I couldn't live with myself for what I did. Eventually, I killed myself.

Floating up and out of his body, he notices the healing beings who surround him. They have come to help him understand more fully the situation that prompted the tragic choice that he faced. He is hesitant but gives them permission to heal him, to help him release the guilt and self-loathing he realizes he has carried forward into Neil's life.

The soul of his brother is called in for him to embrace, but he is so overcome with remorse he is unable to speak. He can sense his brother's forgiveness but is unable to put words to the shame that burns in his heart.

The higher beings are telling me that I must learn to forgive myself. Even though I don't completely understand, I am being told that things happen that are a part of the flow of the divine plan. I understand what I must do.

Neil perceives that he is surrounded by a brilliant healing light. The higher beings are offering release so he might take needed future steps. Ultimately, Neil must accept what happened and why it happened in order to forgive himself.

His session surfaced the beliefs and emotions that had been holding him back for decades in this life. To move ahead and achieve lasting relief, both will need to be balanced.

The higher beings have shown him a clear path forward. It begins with a simple step.

You must let go and release this. It is not serving you.

Many readily acknowledge that earth is a school. Others acknowledge that the curriculum is arduous. But too often, people skip over a corollary fact. If you incarnate on earth to learn and grow, then you are assured to make mistakes. Even people who follow that logic hold unrealistic ideas about accepting their own transgressions. Learning to accept yourself for who you are and for what you've been or done is crucial to forgiving yourself and freeing your future.

Neil's case illustrates an important fact regarding regression therapy. Unlocking the past enables a fuller understanding of what we believe, how it makes us feel, and how we have learned to cope as a result. But effecting long lasting and permanent change requires that we apply this insight to make different choices.

There is no multi-hour session or magic solution that mitigates past suffering. What there is, is clarity about what needs to be replaced and direction about how best to achieve this from the perspective of the higher realms.

* * *

In this next case, we meet Rosalie. For lifetimes spanning centuries, she has carried the heavy burden of responsibility for the harm to others. An encounter with her spiritual figurehead ultimately may lead her to the peace and forgiveness of self that is so deserved.

Rosalie

Rosalie is a 38-year-old single woman who is employed as a dental hygienist. Her relations with her mother and all but one sibling are strained and have been since her father committed suicide thirty years before.

She reached a point several years ago when she recognized that she has built a wall of protection around her heart.

At the point that she scheduled her first regression session, she had significant recall of the details of her current life. But, despite years of therapy, she was still searching for insight into her negative emotions. She chose regression therapy in hopes of achieving lasting emotional relief.

Prior to the experience that follows, she had several regressions. She relived tremendous physical, emotional, and sexual abuse in one, bondage and the murder of all of her fellow villagers in another, and the torture and death of herself and her trusted guardians in a third. Although these lifetimes crossed centuries and in detail were different, each has left her feeling responsible for the mistreatment and death of others.

Regressed, Rosalie finds herself moving between two pastoral scenes. In the first, she is recalling a scene earlier in her current life before her father's suicide. But it is the second that proves to be most significant.

> *I was only ten. I tried to be a good girl. I tried not to make trouble. In school, I followed the rules, got good grades. Despite everything, my father killed himself.*

Uncoached, Rosalie moves to a different scene.

> *I am stepping into a garden, there are lots of flowers and trees. It's breathtaking I am a little girl. I see a man walking toward me. It's Jesus. We sit silently for minutes as he pets my little animal companion.*

Rosalie begins to cry.

> *I feel wrapped in a lot of love and peace. Now I am hugging him. He is telling me I am loved. He tells me to let go of the pain, it could not have been any other way.*
>
> *I need to forgive myself. There is no need for me to keep punishing myself. I have been blaming myself for my father's suicide. Everything came crashing down. I felt responsible for the debacle that followed. The illusion of a happy family was shattered. We lost the security of having a provider, all of us had to focus on how we were going to survive.*

It wasn't my fault. I was only ten. I was an innocent child. He was supposed to be protecting me, protecting us. Instead, I felt I had to protect my siblings. All of this forced me to grow up fast.

My trust was shattered, and my spirit was crushed.

After that, I was always focused on hiding, protecting myself.

Rosalie makes reference to the three lifetimes that she feels responsible for the many who suffered, even though the mistreatment was exacted by others.

I still don't feel like a heroine for rescuing my siblings. Nor did I in any of the prior lives in which others lost their lives. I carry the guilt for their deaths.

Rosalie recalls a life in Scotland in the 1200s. Her name is Elise.

Elise's life is the best example. Her attempt to secure her grandfather's help to rescue the villagers ended in disaster. Instead, he killed them all. I was left feeling responsible for their deaths.

Doing the right thing does not always turn out well. It can result in pain, misery, and even death for others. That's a very high price to pay!

Jesus responds to Rosalie's self-incriminations.

For every positive, there is a negative. Light, shadow, good, bad, each of these have to be balanced. Unfortunately, the bad counterbalances the good, as shadow counterbalances the light. You need to understand that bad things happen. As long as the intention was good, you should forgive yourself. No one is beyond God's acceptance and love.

Comforted by his words, Rosalie spends her last few minutes wrapped in the peace, acceptance, and love Jesus exudes.

Jesus' words echo for some time.

Let go of the pain, it could not have been any other way.

The insight gained pinpoints the beliefs that Rosalie must release to achieve resolution. For more than 30 years, despite putting an end to the mistreatment of her siblings, she blamed herself for her father's suicide, the family's loss of financial security, and the ensuing emotional fracturing. Rather than see herself as a courageous young girl, she has been racked by guilt and grief. Her falsely held belief that she was responsible caused tremendous pain over the decades. The coping mechanisms she developed exerted their own price.

Not able to trust, she walled herself off from family and built emotional barricades that precluded forming a long-term, committed relationship. In an effort to protect, she applied an emotional anesthetic that has robbed her of happiness and love.

If she is able to follow Jesus' advice and to form new beliefs, she will come to understand that she has mistakenly assumed responsibility for the trauma inflicted on others. In prior lifetimes, she carried guilt for the heinous treatment of others by her murderous grandfather in one life, her sociopathic husband in another, and the crusaders in a religious war. In this lifetime, she has wrongly carried responsibility and guilt for the actions and inactions of her parents.

Like so many, Rosalie has struggled to understand the duality of the earth realm, where balance teeters between positives and negatives. Her tendency to displace responsibility from others has caused great suffering and caused her to close her heart.

Only time will tell whether the comfort and acceptance of her spiritual figurehead are enough for her to rewrite the beliefs that were formed centuries before and reinforced in multiple lifetimes since then. Inner peace is within her reach if she can do so. Buoyed by her devotion and clarity about previously confused beliefs, again, Jesus' words echo.

Let go of the pain, it could not have been any other way.

Our whole spiritual transformation brings us to the point where we realize that in our own being, we are enough.

—RAM DASS

5

Self-Acceptance and Doubt

Your opinions about yourself begin to be shaped in your early days. First by parents and other family members, then by friends, neighbors, teachers, and religious figures. Later, the views of coworkers, other members of your communities, the media, and society-at-large cascade.

The sheer volume of messages about who and what you should be, how you should feel and how you should act is astounding. Although for some, this barrage rolls like the proverbial water off a duck's back, others are deeply impacted, rendering them constantly doubting their thoughts, feelings, and actions.

It is a fairly common experience to look back on something you have done or said and decide that it was unacceptable. But if internal critics have taken up permanent residence in your life, it may be time for you to evict them. If you are not your own source of validation and acceptance, most likely you are cheated out of inner calm. A starting point is to understand that what others say is about them and not about you. As you progress on your spiritual path, you will become more reliant on your inner compass and find equanimity.

What do you say about yourself?

* * *

In the cases that follow, you will see how the beliefs held by internal critics cause significant emotional distress and steal peace and joy.

Gwen

Gwen is a 50-year-old woman who recently celebrated her 20th wedding anniversary. After twenty-five years as an actress, she transitioned to teaching drama to aspiring actors. Despite her talent and beauty, she is insecure and often doubts herself.

She has been struggling to shatter a belief that she needs to lead her life according to the standards that society has established.

Gwen scheduled her regression sessions in hopes of resolving a number of searing emotional issues, including prolonged grief over the death of her former lover, Jack, who she knew as a soul intimate from prior lifetimes. She is seeking to reach self-acceptance and forgiveness. She is also hoping to gain insight into her fear of driving.

Gwen believed that she had brought closure to the relationship with Jack, which ended more than two decades ago, but found herself stuck in sadness and regret. These feelings were complicated by guilt for having loving feelings for both Jack and her husband. Fearing that her husband might not understand, she had been hiding her grief about Jack's death from him, pretending that all was right with the world.

Gwen experiences two lifetimes during her past life regression. During the first, she is a child living on a rice farm in Japan in the 1930s and 1940s. Despite life challenges, her childhood is filled with an abundance of love, ease, and peacefulness.

As a young child, named Sha-sha, she sees herself as the center of both her mother and grandmother's attention. Both love her deeply. Two different people, unconditionally loving the same baby, no competition between them.

Love rippling out, not needing to be apportioned.

I am reveling in the laughter and smiles. I love them both. My love for one doesn't negate my love for the other. I am happy to be loved by both of them.

> *I just want to get more of it. I am enjoying it all. I am enjoying this sense of love and attention.*
>
> *There is an ease and sweetness to life. Life can be so peaceful, even though meeting survival needs is difficult for my parents. Despite the harshness of life, I am able to focus on the good, not on the more challenging or bad aspects.*

The higher self is joined by her spirit guide. His name is Ishtok. He shares his view of the challenges.

> *The peace, joy, and love enveloping Sha-sha is such a contrast to the sadness that is all too common in Gwen's current and earlier lives. She is wrapped-up in guilt and shame, despite the purity of her soul. No matter what life she goes into, she is carrying shame and guilt. This is not the true essence of who she is.*
>
> *Sha-sha's purity and innocence are reminders of the simplicity and joy, the playfulness of her eternal nature. She is meant to connect to the peacefulness and love in life. She is meant to live without guilt and shame.*

To glean a full understanding of what is fueling beliefs of guilt and shame and a belief that love can be impure, I move Gwen through time. We briefly visit a lifetime in the late 19th century in which she lived as a prostitute in a western town. She was aware that life circumstances left her with no control over her life. Nothing else was uncovered.

Once again, I prompt Gwen to move to the first time when she came to believe that love is impure. She arrives in a life in ancient Egypt. She is a beautiful young girl named Jezeez who lives a privileged life. As is customary within noble families, she is expected to marry her brother and is not free to partner with the person she desires.

With a sense of dread and obligation, she is schooled in the ways of pleasure and what is expected of her sexually during a week of celebration and pampering. She is aware that she enjoys the pampering and attention but conflicted given her sexual attraction and fantasies of being together with Jada, who is a servant of the house. Class barriers and her compliance with family expectations preclude this union. Squelching a sense of independence and adventure, she suppresses her own desires.

I didn't really want this life with my brother. I did not feel that way about him. I acquiesced and conformed. This was my first inkling of wanting something different, something other than what society dictated.

I move Jezeez ahead, and she sees herself at 29 years old. With an embarrassed laugh, she says that she watched her brother mature and grow to become a handsome man. She is quick to add that he *is no longer a boy.*

She describes living as a normal, happy couple with two children but admits that during the early years of marriage she fantasized about Jada when she made love to her husband.

It made it more okay to have to make love with my brother. I was conflicted. I wanted to live up to the ideals and social expectations. There was a part of me that wanted to have sexual feelings for my husband, but I just couldn't allow myself. Despite the societal expectations and approval, there was no way I could. I didn't feel it was right to be forced to couple rather than to couple naturally.

When asked who Jada might be in Gwen's current life, she identifies him as Gwen's first love Jack. It seems the passage of thousands of years has not stifled the memories of unrealized longing and love.

When moved to the last day of her life, she's 59 and ill with tuberculosis. Her husband was lost at sea several years before. She'd settled into her roles as mother and grandmother, which were rigid and limiting. She did not remarry due to social expectations. She was aware that she had long ago given up any belief that she could have a love life of her own making.

After dying, the higher self reflects back on Jezeez's life.

I didn't feel capable of acting out. I was scared to be my own person. I have sorrow that I chose always to conform to expectations. I was bound, it was like being in your own little prison. I had no freedom. My life was so well programed that it didn't feel like mine alone. It was so controlled that I couldn't even have my own thoughts.

Despite a comfortable well-to-do life, I felt so alone. I didn't have a deep relationship with my husband. I couldn't express my true feelings and desires.

I wanted a different life, yet I was conflicted because my life was so privileged. It was a good life socially, but I wanted it to be different. There was a lot of emotional repression. I wasn't free to dream or even to have my own thoughts. I couldn't think or imagine that my life could have been different, and that filled me with sorrow.

I can see that in the future I will want a life with freedom, to counterbalance Jezeez's life of constraint and discontent. Societal expectations and restrictions will not dominate. I will want a life in which I am free to think for myself, to dream and to make my own decisions.

She is reminded that in her life as Sha-sha, she was loved unconditionally by more than one person. She is left with a new understanding that in the future she will be free to live in freedom, beyond the rigid boundaries of society. She wants to be free to love and express love without constraint and without the weight of guilt or sorrow.

Upon awakening, Gwen is pleased with the messages embedded in the lives she visited.

I loved the message of Sha-sha's life, the absolute simplicity of her life and the sense of appreciation of life. By contrast, I have trouble grasping that in my current life. This reminder is so fundamental.

She continues.

Jezeez could not live outside the box of society's expectations for her. I can relate this to wanting to have my own thoughts and to freely choose my own identity.

Even though social constructs are loosening, when I think about loving both Jack and my husband, I realize that the three of us are bound within the same social construct. Jealousy is a natural by-product. Within this paradigm there is no room for the idea that you can love two men at the same time.

Jezeez's experience has highlighted the issue of self-acceptance.

I definitely struggle with deep sorrow. Even in this life, I feel like I always have to have a happy face. I never feel like I can show it. If I express my sorrow, it will hurt others' feelings. Upon learning of Jack's death, I couldn't let my husband see me grieving. Even though he would have understood, I couldn't risk hurting him.

Gwen seems to believe that if she is truthful about her feelings, she might be no longer loved, that she would be forsaken or banished. She will have to work to uncover what additional beliefs she holds so that she can step into her own power without harming others.

As hoped, Gwen's past life regression has provided fertile ground for exploration in her life between lives session.

Returning the following month for her LBL, Gwen easily goes into trance and briefly revisits a life as a woman called Frances. By her own description, she accomplished little in her short life, dying in an auto accident at 27 and delaying going into the light for five years. The crash, caused by another driver, carried a lesson about what can happen when one does not have or exert control over oneself.

Once in the interlife, her higher self is joined by her guide, Ishtok. He begins a long description of past challenges and his hopes for Gwen's life.

There is a part of Gwen that would prefer not going out into the world, she likes to sequester herself. In part, it is to shield her discomfort and other fears. The body chosen by her higher self is sensitive to stimulation. It is a nervous and anxious body. This contributes to her fear of driving.

But the fear of driving is intended to be overcome. She is supposed to gain confidence in herself and her abilities. If she can overcome this fear, she will know she can overcome other fears. It will boost her confidence.

I am trying to assure her that this is the time to let go. This is not the time to be controlling. She needs to be at peace. She need not fear that her life will be cut short again. There are countless opportunities to live and grow.

Frances' earlier death reinforced caution and framed the belief that if you are not conscious, fully awake, and aware, you might not grow in the way you were supposed to grow, including spiritually. This has rendered Gwen overly cautious.

Ishtok continues.

Frances missed opportunities in her short life. She skated along, living a nice, happy life filled with parties and dancing, but she lacked depth. Her lifetime was a counterpoint to the harshness of her prior life as a prostitute. Being in survival mode made it hard to be reflective and thoughtful during that lifetime.

Her higher self planned for Gwen to get it right, to strike the right balance. Gwen needs more balance and variety in her life. She needs to do things that are fun, playful, and out of the ordinary routine of her life so that she can feel more joyful. Her seriousness reflects her eternal nature and will help her to grow spiritually.

Power is indeed a theme running through Gwen's different lifetimes. There is a part within her that needs to embrace her own power, and to do it in a way that doesn't harm others, in a way that she will feel good about herself.

She needs to assume authority over herself. And she needs to believe that she can take care of herself. She gives a lot of her power up to other people, especially men. And she gives up her power to the belief that she is incapable of doing things. She forfeits her own power due to her lack of confidence without trying.

Frances' car accident was planned as a wake-up event, to trigger becoming more serious about her spiritual pursuits. More specifically, the crash caused by another driver was meant to symbolize what can happen when one does not have or exert control over oneself.

Gwen does not yet believe that she has what it takes to have authority over herself. That belief was formed in her life as Jezeez. All the beliefs she struggles with are intertwined—social obligation, conformity, acceptance, control. Jezeez had no authority in that life. She had no ability to make important decisions. Although understandable given life circumstances at that time, she didn't question even her ability to make a different life for herself.

This is a huge theme for her that comes up time and time again. She doesn't grasp control of her life and then ends up being controlled by others. She spent many lives as a woman in patriarchal societies. Typically, she acquiesces to that. Although she wouldn't like to, it would do her good to choose a future life as a man.

She believes she has to have a romantic relationship. They can become a helpful forum for her to learn about her likes and dislikes, and to ultimately discover how these relationships help or hinder her to express herself.

But she has been challenged to accept her power and authority in relationships in this life. This is a part of her soul's plan for this lifetime. In the future, it will likely be accomplished through taking small steps.

Gwen doesn't trust herself; in part because she hasn't had the ability to make autonomous decisions. She had too many lives in which she was subjugated by men. This has reinforced doubt and undercut her self-acceptance. But it is important for her to learn to trust herself. Because of this, I am not allowed to give her much ongoing guidance in order to help with this.

When she does make decisions, she often criticizes herself for what unfolds. Her doubts and lack of trust are impediments. She will benefit from recognizing the value of making decisions, even if they are wrong or have negative outcomes. Mistakes will be made along the way but are a part of becoming more accepting of herself, as well as accepting of the fact that there will be grief, sadness, and other negative emotions in life.

She can free herself from incrimination.

In lifetime after lifetime, Gwen has been dismissive of herself. This is a habit that will need to be broken for her to restore balance. Softening her self-critique and judgement is her path to self-acceptance and self-love. She has many qualities and accomplishments to be proud of. Honoring those will provide her the peace and joy she so deserves as she works toward that goal.

After a lengthy discourse on love and self-love, Ishtok called in the soul of Jack, Gwen's beloved first love. In their energetic embrace, Gwen hears him whisper *I love you.*

Gwen has received a gift that will live on for a long time, a reminder from the astral realm that love never dies. Only time will tell whether this will help to lessen her grief. But one thing is certain, when she transitions to the afterlife, Jack will be among those waiting for a loving embrace.

Gwen's session was rich in insight about the threads of her emotional distress and discontent. Hiding her sadness over Jack's death for fear of upsetting her husband intensified her grief. Gaining an understanding about the origin of this constraint freed her to begin the healing process in earnest.

Gwen has paid a dear price for choosing to live within the boundaries of others' views and expectations. Ishtok's analysis left no doubt of the challenges to be overcome. Her journey forward will be fueled by her desire to replace doubt with confidence. As she learns to trust herself and be guided by her own desires and opinions, the freedom that she enjoys will counter the risks she endures. Remembering that this is earth school and that mistakes are inevitable will be important as she begins to learn to forgive and accept herself.

Forsaking ourselves in order to conform to others' expectations is a choice fraught with emotional danger. To avoid this pitfall, it is important to constantly ask yourself—to whom have you ceded your authority. Who is occupying rent free space in your mind or heart? When you uncover who they are, it would serve you well to decide whether the time is right for you to evict them.

* * *

In the next section you will meet, Cecelia. Like Gwen, her doubt, lack of self-acceptance, and other limiting beliefs about herself were formed thousands of years ago. Likely, they were reinforced in lifetimes since then. As she planned her upcoming life, Cecelia's higher self orchestrated their resurfacing, so any fallacies would become clear. This is an initial step in reformulating more accurate beliefs, which in turn lead to more positive feelings and behaviors.

CECELIA

Cecelia is a 56-year-old pediatric nurse practitioner, plagued by insecurities, including doubt and low self-worth and self-acceptance. She believes she has not realized her potential in life, and this causes her significant distress. These sentiments have contributed to financial challenges, which have added another layer of stress to her life. She underwent her regression session hoping to understand the spiritual lessons embedded within these trials and find a path to healing.

Once regressed, she arrives in a beautiful garden where she encounters her higher self, whose eternal name is Grace. Grace comments that she was prepared for the challenges that would unfold in her life as Cecelia.

I knew it would be tough. I wanted to take on something important and big, so I knew it would not be an easy life.

Grace begins to describe a life as a young woman, Veronica, several thousand years ago. She encounters a powerful officer during Roman times on a trek to fetch water. Astride his horse, he blocks her path. She does not feel threatened but is somewhat confused by his attention. She senses his interest is sexual but at 15 has no experience to guide her. Moving ahead somewhat in time, she relives their first sexual encounter.

I'm not fighting it. I'm aware that I am conflicted, both enjoying the encounter but not sure it is okay. It's the first time for me. He's awakening sexual feelings in me, but no one has prepared me for this. Even though he's attracted to me, I don't know if there is anything beyond that, as he's married.

Sex was uncomfortable, but I liked being held. I enjoyed the attention. I had positive feelings for him. I didn't think it was okay, because he belonged to someone else. I became ashamed of it.

Despite doubts and her own belief that it was wrong, Veronica continued the affair until it was exposed by the officer's wife. There was a public shaming within the community for Veronica but not the officer. Although other girls married between 14 and 16, she was ruined by the exposure. Moving ahead several years, she saw herself poor and shunned by the community.

People stopped talking to me. Men didn't want to be with me, or to pursue marriage. My family blamed me, they lost face. It was bigger in their heads than it was in reality, just like it was bigger in my head.

I was very angry. No one stood up for me. I was betrayed, including by my own family.

Since she was banished by her family and community and without any friends, she spends several years caring for elderly and sick people to meet basic needs. Weak and exhausted, she dies at 28.

Her awareness expands as she floats out of her body.

I love it. I can shoot through the whole sky. I am full of energy. I feel light. It makes me wonder why people are so afraid of death.

Her higher self identifies the officer and his wife as two people who have played major roles in her current life.

Life was disappointing. I saw that people had things that I wanted—friends, children, and happiness. I must not have deserved to have what they had. I felt left behind, cast aside. I felt that I was worthless, not worthy. I punished myself. I did not show myself any mercy.

Looking back, if I had made a different decision, none of that would have happened. It was so confusing. I didn't mean any harm.

I had no one to counsel me. No one was saying, it's part of life, it's not going to work, but you are not a bad person. Because it turned out so badly, it made me doubt myself. The doubt was debilitating. I felt powerless. I believed what others were saying about me.

Cecelia is holding onto this old belief. She feels that she is not worthy and that she deserves punishment. She can't accept herself.

As most humans, Veronica had sought love and validation. Instead, the attention she received from the officer resulted in rejection, isolation, and shame. Her confusion turned to self-blame, doubt, and a belief that she didn't deserve even a life of security, joy and worth.

Grace elaborates.

Cecelia doesn't feel safe. The world doesn't feel safe to her. Her lack of financial security is part of it. And part of it is her bad experiences with men have left her afraid. She needs to trust that she's enough, she's more than enough. She's a beautiful soul.

Grace recognizes what Veronica was unable to see in her life and now understands that this lack of understanding has cascaded across lifetimes through two millennia.

Her relationship with the officer was a natural desire for validation and love, both are basic human needs. That is not a disgusting thing, it's a beautiful thing. It is not something that should cause such huge regret. Cecelia can fly with this awareness. I am going to help Cecelia achieve what she deserves—financial security, travel, good relationships, and a flourishing practice.

Armed with this insight and with the support of her higher self, Cecelia can begin work to release the doubt and lack of self-acceptance. These are a preface to formulating new beliefs about herself.

To bolster Cecelia's chance of success, I acknowledge the presence of Archangel Rafael who has joined Cecelia to release the energetic residue from her Roman lifetime. Within a few minutes, she showed visible signs of relief.

In the counseling session that followed, Cecelia shared how she now recognizes an almost parallel set of circumstances unfolded earlier in her current life.

At 11, she began babysitting for a neighborhood family. Both husband and wife showered love and attention on her, treating her like one of their own children. Over time, the attention took a sordid turn. The wife began dressing Cecelia up to look like a young adult, teaching her how to fix her hair and wear make-up. The pair introduced her to men who viewed her as a sexual object. The husband became flirtatious, and when she was 15, he became more sexual. Their behavior elicited the same feelings and confusion that Veronica had experienced when she became involved with the handsome officer.

I loved them. I was fascinated by their glamorous life. It was so much more exciting than my family. When I told my mother, she was very cruel. I felt so sinful. I thought I was going to hell. When I got older and looked back on it, I felt like I had ruined my life. In my early thirties, I tried to contact him to find out why this had happened and learned that he'd died.

Years later, I joined a women's group which helped me to cope with all that had happened. I reached a point when I was able to hold those who had mistreated me accountable and understand the role I played in both situations.

Cecelia accomplished this first level of healing by coming to terms with the external circumstances that had caused her to doubt herself. What she had yet to do before her regression was recognize her intrinsic value and worth.

Her regression uncovered the beliefs that she'd internalized several thousand years before, chief among them are beliefs that she is not worthy of having a good life, and worse yet; that she deserves to be punished. Likely, her doubt, lack of self-acceptance, and other limiting beliefs about herself were reinforced in lifetimes since then. As she planned her upcoming lifetime, Cecelia's higher self orchestrated the resurfacing of these false beliefs. As their fallacy became clear, Cecelia was positioned to formulate more accurate beliefs.

Once uncovered, they still needed to be replaced. The clarity she gained and the healing release that she received have placed her in a much stronger position to succeed at the work that remains.

New beliefs need to be formed. Chief among them is the conviction that she has intrinsic value and worth, despite any mistake in the past or the future. She needs to accept the past and what it has taught her.

* * *

Next, we meet Terry, who like Cecelia journeys across millennia to uncover the circumstances that have fostered and reinforced doubt and lack of acceptance. In her journey to the interlife, she is buoyed by the unconditional acceptance and loving advice of loved ones.

Terry

Terry is 60 years old with two adult children who she is very close to. She is distraught about her husband's recent decision to divorce her after their decades long marriage, despite the fact that she has considered leaving him for some time. She is no stranger to loss, having coped with the death of her sister and her first-born child. She is hoping to understand the fears and doubt that for too long have paralyzed her, one of which is that there is never ample money.

In her past life regression, Terry experiences a life several thousand years ago in Egypt as a member of the ruling family. She had been exiled and most tragically had lost all contact with her children. Like other women at the time, she had no control over her life. She was powerless and felt worthless. She was loved, but in her own words, *no one loved her enough to save her.* Her voice quickened with anxiety and dread as she recalled an important moment.

> *I am in a boat. It's dark, an inky black. We are trying to reach safety, but we don't. Now I am in the water. It's too late. I drowned, along with many others.*

As she floats out of her body and connects to her higher self, she begins to calm down. She notices that she is immersed in pastel blues and pinks, reminiscent of her experience in deep meditative states. She relaxes in the safety and love that the colors have come to represent.

> *The colors are so beautiful. I feel so much lighter. I know I am safe now.*
>
> *My sister is here. She's always been pure love, but so am I. She's telling me I am not alone and that I am okay. I feel very comforted by her. She's telling me I'm going to be okay. I'm not to be afraid. It's just an illusion.*

The presence of Terry's sister, who died more than 20 years ago, momentarily calmed her. But soon, she reflects on the many loved ones she has lost.

> *Everybody is leaving because I am not good enough. This belief was shaped long before. I was supposed to take care of people, and then I couldn't, so it's my fault. I didn't take care of the things and the people that I was supposed to take care of. I could have if they let me.*

She is helped to look at her current life.

> *I am just not sure what I am supposed to do next. I have to trust myself more. I am really smart, but I lose sight of this. Even though I have succeeded, I doubt the results. I doubt my abilities. I am not good enough. Somebody told me that, and I believed it. She repeats this last statement multiple times with great emphasis.*
>
> *I know that it's time to stop believing this.*

From this higher perspective, Terry is shown that she is holding onto these limiting beliefs. In an effort to uncover their origin, we attempt to look back on the life that has just ended. Instead, she recalls a second life that also ended tragically.

I just died. I was burned to death, they believed we were witches. They killed all of us. They thought we were a threat. I didn't do anything wrong. I'm not enough. I had children then also, but the ones who killed me didn't care. We were all innocent. It's not okay what they have done. It's not good.

I'm surrounded by yellow, pink and white shapes. The shapes are my friends. They love me. They are souls who watch me. My sister is also here. She's going to take me to a better place. She is so good. She is pure love.

Terry's focus switches back to her current life.

My sister is telling me to move to California, where my children live. Now, with the divorce, there is no impediment. She's reminding me that I feel safe and loved with them. Perhaps they are the same children that I lost in those past two lives.

I ask Terry if the loved ones who have gathered to comfort her can offer insight about her belief that she *is not enough*. She elaborates after noting that her full understanding will unfold slowly.

It's not one specific answer. It's going to come to me little by little. I have to have patience and trust. I am getting closer to understanding. I grasp it, but it slips out of my hands. It includes me feeling safe, as I do when I am with my son and daughter.

After noting that her husband did not make her feel safe, even though it was something she wanted, Terry acknowledged that he is carrying out his soul contract.

He's just doing his job, playing the role as we agreed.

The spirits who showed themselves to Terry comforted her and reminded her of how protected she is. She was uplifted with their encouragement and love.

> *There's an amazing amount of love that they want me to take back with me. It can't leak out, it can't escape. The task ahead is exhausting, but not overwhelming. I have to pay attention to everything. It can be fun. It doesn't have to be so painful.*

No sooner had the loving and encouraging spirit voices faded, Terry connected to a life in which she was a family man name Jacob, whose life was upended.

> *I've made choices that were not wise. I was greedy and embezzled funds. I lied to my wife about where the money came from. I thought I had to steal to provide the comfortable life I believed my family deserved. Also, I was mean and did not treat my wife or children well. I was so ashamed. After I was released from jail, I couldn't face them. I couldn't go home. Eventually, I ended up as a beggar, living in alleys, mistreated by those who passed by. I died in the street.*
>
> *I'm not going to let that happen again. I have to have more money so that I don't die on the street again. I wouldn't have been in the situation if I had more money. I am afraid in the future I might do it again if I don't think I have enough money.*
>
> *I guess I got what I deserved!*

In her brief reflection on that life, Terry gained insight about her insecurity about money, an issue she identified as being key to the dissolution of her current marriage. She connected that belief to her desire that her husband assume financial responsibility for her despite her own earning power.

> *I didn't want to take a chance that I wouldn't have enough. Jacob's life ended tragically because he didn't have enough money to care for himself. I was afraid that it would happen again, so I depended too much on my husband.*

For Terry, fear and insecurity converged in Jacob's life with her insecurity and belief of not measuring-up. This combination further deepened her self-doubt and self-condemnation.

Fortunately, with the assistance from higher beings, Jacob was reminded that souls incarnate in the earth school to learn lessons and that mistakes of judgement and actions are among the outcomes. He was told that we are loved despite small or large blunders. He was reminded that he is not bad. Wrapped in unconditional love and acceptance, he found forgiveness for himself and from those who had carried his suffering forward. His closing words reflect his gift to Terry—a life with freedom to live without fear or doubt.

Terry's session has already shifted her perspective and lifted the weight of long held false beliefs.

> *I'm definitely good enough. I am not going to forget it this time. They are saying that they are going to stay with me. There is so much more work to do. I have to go to California. There is something out there for me, but they aren't telling me what it is.*

Terry prepares to end the session, knowing that as she moves ahead, she will be fueled by their love and unconditional acceptance.

> *I am part of them also. It is sad to leave them. That's why I cry a lot. I'm not afraid anymore, at least not so much. I can be so funny. They want me to express that more often, to be playful and joyful. It will ease the work that lies ahead for me to accomplish.*
>
> *I am being told to believe in the power of the human spirit. I've heard this before in a dream. I am being showered by bright, pulsating lights that are all around.*
>
> *I have to hold onto the truth that there is more than just this experience here on earth. Earth life is not permanent. I will be leaving this experience someday like a play that comes to an end. I can see that the experience never really changes who I am, a being of love who is loved by countless other beings. I have always been that. I can feel that when I am with my children. They are the strongest link to this deep sense of love and acceptance.*

Terry's session prepared her to come to terms with the divorce. While it did not wash away her sadness, it muffled the distorted script that she was running about herself. The pattern that unfolded across three lifetimes fostered her fears, insecurities, and overwhelming self-doubt. The voices of those who know, love, and accept her drowned out the falsities that were running her internal monologue.

Clearly, the path forward will require time and additional work. Grief does not respond to our desire that it quickly end. But her new understanding empowers her as she faces the difficult days ahead.

In the months following her session, Terry can use these insights she gleaned for the hard work of forming new beliefs. Once she does, she will notice how much better she will feel, and how motivating these positive feelings about herself become. Armed with them, she will be in a much better position to make different choices in the future.

The fresh memories of the eternal state of love and unconditional acceptance that we return to after each lifetime will buoy her during difficult moments. She concluded her session knowing that she can retrieve this loving connection when she quiets her mind and emotions during meditation.

* * *

The next case illustrates how the release that occurs in a regression session continues beyond the end of the session. In the experience of Sheila, who we meet next, her session led to an outpouring of thoughts and emotions from years of nonacceptance by her parents. Her candor and first-hand description of the pain she carried for so long shows the damage incurred when we are not accepted by those we love. Sheila's willingness to share her understandings demonstrate the therapeutic value of releasing falsely held beliefs.

SHEILA

Sheila is 60 years old and has lived with her partner Christina for the last 20 years. She scheduled her past life regression session hoping to gain a deeper understanding of emotional sticking points, including fear.

Once Sheila is in trance, I direct her to go to the lifetime that will uncover the origin of her fear.

Sheila finds herself living in a primitive desert environment in ancient times. She is a young girl, Selia, who is responsible for getting water from the well.

Anyone who tries to do something different gets punished. You must adhere to the rules and stay in your role. It's important for our collective survival in this harsh environment. There are many dangers, so women must be protected. I heard stories of people who ventured out. They told us these stories to instill fear. If you try to do something different, there is humiliation and physical punishment. You are rejected by everyone.

I wish I was free to do something different. I look at the ocean and see the boats go out. I dream about going out on the boats to explore. But it's impossible. I am forever tied to this village. The idea of breaking out is impossible.

When I was 5 years old, I was given a chore, but I decided to do something else. I was distracted by a lamb. I was curious to see where it was going, so I followed it out of the village. They came for me, and they hit me and yelled at me to never do it again. Then I was confined. It made a huge impression on me. I never explored again. I never wanted to displease the elders.

Digging deep into her eternal memories, Sheila's higher self has pinpointed the beliefs that have constrained her.

I have felt frustrated for a long time because of the confining roles that I have been put in, in some instances because the dangers were too significant and in other instances the opportunities were not there. The need to conform to others' expectations and the belief that it wasn't safe was repeatedly reinforced. Women were not treated well. I was always afraid. Bad things will happen if I break out and venture too far.

And now we shift to hear from Sheila about the insights that flowed in the days following her session.

The morning after the regression, I woke up and knew that the body of water that Selia lived near was the Red Sea. Looking on the internet, I recognized the color of the ground, the ancient ruins, the water, and the shoreline.

The floodgates of information and emotion opened.

In this village where I lived as Selia, each person had a role, and a person couldn't waver from that role. Everyone's survival depended on it. Selia's job was to carry heavy water jugs from a well, up a hill, and along a dusty path to the village. Water was needed for all sorts of things to meet the needs of the villagers. Water was precious. She was very strong, and proud of her strength.

Even though she was proud of her ability, Selia wanted to do something else. In the moments when she was allowed to take a break, she would walk down to the edge of the sea and watch the boats come in and go out. She would stare out at the sea and dream of going out on one of the boats to explore. If she could, she would never come back. But she knew it was a futile dream because only the men were sea merchants and seafarers.

The punishment Selia received for exploring was so severe that it made a lasting impression on her. She never disobeyed the rules again. As time passed, her frustration built. She believed she was trapped. She hated being in a preordained role with no other opportunity nor creative outlet.

My life as Selia made a deep and lasting impression on me. I think I vowed never to allow myself to be trapped in a role that didn't suit me or allow me to be myself. I was never satisfied, even though I loved the sea, the landscape, and friends and family.

In my current life, I needed to develop courage to break out of preordained roles that culture and society have placed on me. I feel like I've had many lives since Selia's in which I've tried to do better and find a way to break out, but I haven't quite succeeded. I'm sure some lives I've done better than others with this lesson.

In my current life, I feel as if obstacles were put deliberately in my way to see how I would cope with them and what I would do about them. Would I go along and acquiesce like Selia did and keep my frustrations and longings to myself, or would I take the risk and make my own path, despite the consequences? Would I be able to forgive and not get bitter and self-destructive, and instead thrive in this life?

I think in past lives I went along and faked it, and I didn't forgive people who wronged me, instead I let the lack of forgiveness destroy me.

Reflecting on my current life, my early years were filled with challenges. My parent's cultural values and religious beliefs are rigid. I endured my father's sexual abuse, who was repeating his own abuse as a child.

My father also had a lot of anger and rage, and it was directed at me. I was thankful that he never drank alcohol because I believe he could have killed us in a drunken rage. My mother was no help and set a poor example of standing up for oneself and for others. She acquiesced, acting like nothing was wrong. She put the best face forward to the public.

After I read about past life regression and life between lives, I sensed that I had chosen to live a life as their daughter as a test and learning experience. The challenge is to strength my self-acceptance.

As a child, I tried to go along to win their approval and praise, but it just wasn't quite right. As I matured, I learned to see the world through a broader lens. They wanted certainty, and I am comfortable with mystery.

It's difficult to spend time with family members when ways of seeing the world are so different. A discordant undercurrent is always there. To keep the peace, I would keep my differing views to myself.

I realized after decades of denying it that I was gay. I didn't admit it to myself until I was 30 years old, after years of loneliness, confusion, shame, and wasted time.

My parents didn't handle this well. My mother blamed herself and said I was going to hell and maybe it would have been better if I had never been born.

Their lack of acceptance was extreme. They resorted to trickery and manipulation, including fooling me into going into a place that claimed to convert gay people. They had me on a prayer chain for years, but at some point gave-up on that.

I reached a point when I had to be willing to be completely out of their lives if necessary because I needed to be authentic and to be a sane, healthy, and productive person. Eventually, they have come to accept that I don't fit their norms. They tolerate me, but don't fully accept me. It hurts.

Sheila had not been allowed to break free of ideological constraints placed on her by others in lifetimes spanning two millennia. As a result, her curiosity and wanderlust were squashed.

Sheila has come to understand that the obstacles she has encountered in this life were not accidental but planful. Even before she learned about the soul planning process, she had a deep knowing that life obstacles were put deliberately in her way to see how she would cope with them.

Despite her stated fears, she has chosen not to acquiesce. Unlike Selia, changing social mores enabled her to be true to herself and to risk the consequences.

> *I think it's natural to go through stages of wanting to fit in with a peer group or to gain parental acceptance. But it is exhausting to have to continuously swim against the cultural currents of the age.*

Sheila has learned to forgive by watching and learning from others' mistakes. She vowed never to let that happen to her. She saw that unforgiveness hurts the unforgiving more than the person who wronged. In her words, *it's possible I've had many lifetimes learning the forgiveness lesson.*

In the future, freely choosing a path of nonconformity will necessitate continuing work to overcome residual fears.

Many can identify with the conditioning that rendered Sheila compliant and willing to live within strict expectations and rules. The freedom to choose how to live is not equally available to all either, by personal or societal circumstances.

Perhaps your life has been limited by the constraints and expectations of others. But perhaps like Sheila, you're determined to accept yourself. If you have not already done so, it may be time for you to determine whether an internal critic is occupying rent free space in your mind and heart and to prepare the eviction.

The only way to inner calm is to become your own source of validation and acceptance. Otherwise, you are not only being cheated out of inner peace, but you risk losing the freedom to chart your own future.

Remember what others say is about them and not about you. As you progress on your spiritual path, reliance on your inner compass flows more naturally.

Stop acting so small. You are the Universe in ecstatic motion.

—RUMI

6

SELF-WORTH

The plan each soul crafts for a lifetime includes myriad opportunities to learn. One of the things commonly included in a life plan is development or refinement of self-worth.

Many understand that our self-worth is influenced by the views of others. While this is true, trauma and other experiences in prior lives may have left the soul holding false beliefs about itself. When this happens, it is necessary for these false beliefs to be embedded in a future life so that a more positive and balanced view can be developed.

Those struggling with low self-esteem may be overly critical and belittle themselves. Some have a tendency to over identify with their weakness while minimizing or totally ignoring their strengths. They may have difficulty accepting their own behavior, particularly when they conclude their actions were a mistake. In the extreme, they cannot forgive themselves.

People who have not yet cultivated a strong self-worth give their authority to others, too often looking to them for assurance and validation. A corollary is that the suggestions and advice of others are perceived as criticism, even when none was intended. In these instances, lacking a positive sense of self leaves them at the mercy of others who may themselves be unkind, unflattering, critical, or, at worst, cruel.

Do you believe you have intrinsic worth, or are you like countless others who believe that they must earn their value?

Believing that you must earn your value is particularly rampant in communities and societies that disproportionately reward production. In these instances, bounty earned can falsely equate with a person's value. Obsessed with produced value, people succumb to becoming *human doings*, losing sight of the fact that they have intrinsic value as human beings. This pattern contributes to stress, which is acknowledged to be one of the biggest, if not the greatest, determinant of disease and illness.

* * *

In the cases that follow, you will see the brilliance of the soul's strategy for correcting the falsely held views formed in prior lives. Righting false beliefs is not automatic and requires that they first be recognized. Very often before it is enhanced, one's low self-worth causes emotional pain. As we have seen before, upheaval and dismay can be powerful motivators for change.

TINA

Tina is a 32-year-old woman who scheduled a transpersonal session with the hopes of gaining insight regarding her future and the dramas that have challenged her over the last fifteen years. Two boyfriends, Trevor and John, died in tragic accidents. She has been physically victimized by three different men. And in her own words, her first business venture failed, despite the benefit of her advanced business education and acumen.

Early in her session, Tina found herself floating without a body in an ethereal space, surrounded by the star filled night sky, amidst a big swirl of galaxies. It is a familiar place where she felt good. Enjoying the sensation of floating, she sensed the presence of another who identified herself as Julie.

> *It feels like we are exactly the same. We are holding hands. We are staring at the galaxies together.*

Tina learns that Julie is part of her soul that is currently living *across the country in another state.* Before incarnating, their soul decided to split its energy and send it into two concurrent incarnations on earth. This is a rare occurrence for souls, who are cautioned by spirit guides that this choice can result in not having enough energy for either to realize the plans that have been set in place for the lifetime. Nonetheless, this is something the higher self decided prior to incarnating. This decision has been forgotten by Tina, like all other aspects of the soul plan she crafted for this lifetime.

Julie, on the other hand, has developed a capacity for out-of-body travel and has visited Tina before. She is hopeful that Tina will also develop this skill. They had made no prior plan to meet in person during their respective lifetimes but had set the intention to connect "in soul state."

Julie's concern for Tina was evident from the outset. In fact, it was she who inspired Tina to pursue spiritual regression. Julie knew that the process could help Tina work through the issues she is struggling with. Julie's perspective regarding Tina's struggles was revealing and would prove invaluable to the insight sought by Tina.

> *I have missed Tina so much. I want her to be happy and to understand that she is not alone. The past is getting in the way of her being happy. She's overwhelmed by the things that happened to her, including the death of both Trevor and John.*
>
> *These relationships were meant to teach her different things. Both were intended to help her along her spiritual journey. Trevor was her first love, he was all fun. Tina's relationship with John was more challenging due to his verbal and occasional physical mistreatment of her. The two relationships contrasted how love can manifest.*
>
> *Now she is supposed to focus on being happy. One of the reasons I am here today is to remind her that she is supposed to be working on being happy. Tina is backing away as a result of the trauma of those losses. She needs to be less guarded but also to refine her capacity for discerning who is trustworthy.*
>
> *Dating can be tough. Loving is worth the risk. BUT it shouldn't be her primary focus!*

She should invest less in dating relationships and more in herself, especially her interior world. Once she does that, love will flow more freely and naturally in external relationships.

Julie acknowledges that as a victim of violence and sexual assault, Tina would have reason to be guarded and unwilling to be open to love.

These experiences were built into her plan. The lessons she can take from them ultimately will protect her. She thought everyone was good. She needs to discern who is good and who is not. She needs to toughen-up to protect herself. She formed these beliefs from past lives leading her to be too trustworthy. She needs to learn to discern trustworthiness. Her relationships with both Trevor and John were intended to help her practice this.

She needs to balance discernment with guardedness, to determine who can be believed. This is a tricky thing to achieve. Tina is practicing discernment at the networking events she attends. But she needs to learn not to be too disappointed when someone turns out not to be trustworthy.

She needs to focus more on her spirituality, to connect more deeply with her eternal nature. If she focuses on interior matters, she will find joy, love, peace, and equanimity. All of this is within her.

Julie elaborates when asked about finding love within.

It starts with yourself, but then it broadens to others. Tina is getting better about focusing on love of self, but she could be better. She has worthiness issues that have been brought in from prior lives. She had a lifetime in Shakespearean times when she was grasping for a man's love. Her emotions obscured her objectivity. She did everything to gain his love, including making many sacrifices. He didn't reciprocate. He turned away. Tina was competing for his attention with his wife and his many lovers.

This lack of worthiness is also impeding her professional success. Tina needs to focus on this before she begins her next venture. She has worked on several business start-ups. They didn't go as planned because she didn't see herself as worthy of success.

Knowing that Tina would benefit from practical advice about how to accomplish this spurred Julie to continue on.

In order to work on her lack of worthiness, she should spend time with children and animals. These 'balls of unconditional love' will help her. She needs to spend more time in nature. It will help ground her in her divine essence. This is the true reality. She will come to understand her true nature. It also will help her to not dwell on others.

I purposely brought her to viewing the night sky before as a reminder of how awe-inspiring nature is. Focusing on this can help her see herself within the grander plan. She needs to stop viewing herself as small and insignificant.

Following an energetic healing provided by unnamed, higher beings, Tina is visited by Trevor. The light-hearted and fun-loving way that he had been described was quite evident in his manner and statements. He joined in to reassure her that she is loved and that he is safe and having fun.

I am in a place, a cloud city. Everything is shiny and pretty. There are tall skyscrapers and brilliant colors and light everywhere. It is heavenly! I have been here since I died on earth. I spend time with pilots, working with them. It is fun. It is helping me to heal the residue from the plane crash. I am working on balancing the trauma from the crash with the fun of flying around with these pilots.

It was my time to leave, dying young was part of my plan. I didn't do it to hurt anyone. People should stop feeling bad that I died young. I am having fun. I am waiting for my friends to come over, I am not planning to incarnate again in the near future.

Before Trevor departs, these young lovers spend quiet minutes wrapped in the presence of each other's love. They have had numerous lifetimes together, including the one cut short. They depart, consoled knowing that they are eternally linked and that their love will never die.

In the counseling session that followed, Tina shared more of the details of prior romantic relationships that connect to her regression.

Sometime after Trevor and John's death, Tina began an on-again, off-again relationship with Hank that spanned seven years. The dynamics were eerily similar to her debilitating affair during her Shakespearean lifetime, the unsatisfied longing due to her lover's infidelity and the necessity for her to set firm boundaries in order not to be swept away by her sexual and emotional impulses. Tina can now see what learning and healing were embedded in that relationship.

Even though we were together in the past, that doesn't mean we need to be together in this life.

She acknowledged that she will need to keep working on feeling good enough about herself so that she doesn't succumb to unbalanced and unsatisfying relationships. She has come to understand that the struggle to resist such advances affords the perfect opportunity to build and strengthen feelings of worthiness.

Grasping for love and attention, in this and prior lifetimes, disempowered her. As Julie was eager to remind her, the emptiness that might be temporarily filled by this type of attention can never fill the yearning for wholeness.

The yearning for wholeness and value is universal and carried across many lifetimes. Many mistakenly look to others to fill this longing when the only permanent fill is within themselves. Connecting to one's intrinsic worth is too often obscured by people and events in the exterior world. And so, developing a strong sense of self takes time and patience.

* * *

As we will see in the next case, the words, actions, and treatment by others can try one's patience, and in the interim, cause much heartache.

Eleanor

Eleanor is 55-years-old and has just celebrated her 15-year mark in an engineering firm. She is happily married to her second husband. After reading *Llewellyn's Little Book of Life Between Lives*, she grew excited about the prospect of connecting to her soul and learning more about her purpose in life.

Eleanor mentioned that one of her challenges is lacking the confidence to speak-up at work. Although she considers herself quite competent, when called upon to discuss the programs that she oversees, she freezes-up. Interestingly, this was neither the focus she hoped to explore in her session nor an issue of great import. She tacked it on the end of our intake conversation. But as has happened with others, it turned out to be an important clue to the wisdom that awaited from the higher realms.

She was surprised to learn in her first past life regression that she had been put to death for killing a woman she believed was responsible for the death of her entire family. In that life, she was a young man nicknamed Brut, who, because of his size and strength, had a reputation and history of being called on to protect people. Ironically, he was unable to save his family, who perished in a fire while he was away protecting others.

He was mocked by his peers, adding fuel to what was a raging emotional cauldron. Distraught and enraged, he lashed out at the woman he suspected was responsible. He was not certain if the girl died, nor did he specifically know what he was being accused of doing, even as he languished in prison. He was certain however that he should be punished for hurting someone. Although he had no recall of killing her, he accepted that he was her killer. He would later learn his assumption was wrong. Although executed for the crime, he was not guilty.

I moved Brut back in time in an effort to understand the origin of his rage. He moved to several years before the fire. He described himself as a warrior who lived a solitary life, apart from the community that he was charged with protecting. Despite his sadness, his position required that he maintain a façade of strength.

> *I look so strong, so people expect me to be strong. I have to live-up to my reputation. I am a protector. I have been called a hero because I was able to defend the fortress. Despite this, I failed to save my family. I should have been there to protect my family. No one else could do it. I could have saved them, but I wasn't there.*
>
> *I can't let people see my feelings of sadness and loneliness and my desire for attention, understanding, and comfort. They look to me as the protector.*

Brut's needs went unmet, while he worked hard to project a false bravado.

Upon his death, Brut was able to speak further about the beliefs that contributed to his sad and tragic life.

If I had saved them, I might not have had so much pent-up rage. I wouldn't have lashed out. Life would not have ended like it had.

I should not have cared so much about what other people thought. If I hadn't, maybe I would have expressed myself more. Understanding and expressing my feelings was difficult. If I thought more positively about myself, I could have had a happier life.

Here were the beliefs that would follow Brut into future lives. The beliefs that the higher self purposely would pack into Eleanor's life plan with the hopes of bringing balance and resolution.

In the next session, Eleanor discussed the insights gleaned from the previous session. She now understood that Brut had been tricked into confessing. His limited cognitive functioning made it easy for the constables to manipulate him. His malleability and inability to speak-up for himself sealed his fate.

I think the point of Brut's story is that he was so totally misunderstood. He didn't know how to handle or express his feelings. He carried such guilt for not saving his family. Then he was mocked for his failure. He was so mired in these feelings that he believed what other people were saying. He was beating himself up. Regardless of what actually happened with the young girl, he said 'I'm guilty, whatever.' The lesson for him was that he shouldn't have cared so much about what others thought. Doing so can be disastrous. He should have thought better of himself.

Discussing her initial reaction to the regression, Eleanor said that the theme resonated with her, noting that she does think too much about what others think.

Part of my inability to express myself is my worry about what others will think of me if I expose myself, including my weaknesses. I worry about how others are judging me. I don't know what I was expecting, but to have this past life story come up was surprising. It showed me the relevance in my current life.

Weeks later, Eleanor was excited to share that she took the message of Brut's life to heart and decided to risk speaking-up at work.

> *I told myself 'okay, this is what it is, this is what I am. I've been working here for 15 years. I have qualities that have value. Some people like me, others may not, but don't be so worried about speaking out.'*

Eleanor was happily surprised that what she had to say was so well received. More importantly, she realized how good it felt to come out of the shadows. Revisiting Brut's painful life had surfaced a deep issue regarding her self-worth. With this first victory to encourage her, she found directionality for the important work that remains.

Emotional and spiritual growth requires accepting yourself for who and what you are. Eleanor's experience is a reminder. Bolstering your self-worth is among the challenges we face in the process of mastering self-love. Brut's experience brought the price paid for not doing so into clear focus.

Like so many others, Eleanor's ideas about her worth have been shaped by others. There was intense pressure to conform during her teens. She was picked on for living in a lovely home and having nice clothes by peers who lived in more economically strained circumstances. She was bullied for getting excellent grades. She was teased for her looks.

> *There were things about me that I couldn't accept. I felt so much pressure. People were cruel. Even though I met other people who thought I was pretty, I didn't believe it enough because of all those years that I was picked on. I worried about what people thought. My own sense of self took some time to develop and was impacted by those experiences.*
>
> *I struggled to fit in. I can't say that I felt good about myself or that I was on my own list. There was no such list in my earlier years. I am pleased to be at a place now where I am more important to myself. Now I am on my list.*

Despite early progress on that front, Eleanor continues to work on trusting herself.

> *I am always looking for a guide to show me the way.*

During her second regression, Eleanor found herself in a garden with Lauren, her higher self. Lauren was displaying a brilliant jewel-embedded gold crown near her heart. Descriptors of the image and the sensations it elicits flowed.

> *I see a prince, a king, his majesty, the majesty within.*
>
> *There is just love now. I want to feel what it's like to be her. I feel like I am merging with her. I look at my body and feel my robes and my hands. The light shines outward. It beams out from the crown, upward and downward. It's beautiful. I am seeing out through her eyes.*
>
> *I am just enjoying the feeling of the crown within my chest and the light beaming out. It's the Christ within.*

Separating, Lauren begins to move away. Her parting words remind Eleanor that they are never apart.

> *There are no other words, I just feel her love.*

Discussing the regression, Eleanor later remarked that the reminder that divinity is within was quite a powerful message. She acknowledged that she still needs to work on self-esteem until she no longer thinks or says anything about herself that she would not think or say about God.

Eleanor is not alone in recognizing that she does not yet treat herself the way she would treat God. For her, the future work is to uncover the beliefs that prevent her from fully realizing her divine essence.

She shared that on her way home from the previous session, a song by a favorite Christian artist was playing with the refrain "what have I done to deserve love like this."

> *This is such a powerful song. The words resonate for me and are so reinforcing. Brut didn't know that God loved him. When Brut died, I saw him clothed in brilliant light and engulfed in his mother's love and unconditional acceptance. I wonder this love that God has for me, what did I do to deserve it?*

Eleanor was shown a life that very dramatically illustrated what can happen when someone doesn't have a strong self-worth and is unable to speak their truth. Like Brut, her sense of self was shattered by the beliefs of others. Blind to all of this, Brut suffered. For Eleanor, a different ending is possible. With the insights gleaned from her sessions, she says that she is now better prepared to uncover the beliefs that are preventing her from walking in the confidence and joy of her connection with her divine essence.

* * *

Challenges to self-worth manifest in many ways and may remain hidden until you dive deep through the pain to understand the embedded lessons. Such is the case for Angelina, the next person we meet.

Angelina

Angelina is 60 years old and has remained single after divorcing more than 20 years ago. She has one adult daughter with whom she is very close. For years, she was very satisfied being single, but in the past few years she has begun to open to the idea of finding a romantic partner.

She overcame early years of poverty to achieve financial security through characteristic endurance. The latter quality helped her to withstand the harsh family environment in which physical punishment and emotional abuse were extreme. Although she physically survived the mistreatment, she did not fare as well emotionally.

She has done several past life regressions and a life between lives session in an effort to release trapped anger and pain that has burdened her since childhood. She hoped to understand what her soul wanted to achieve by selecting her birth family and the abuse that dominated it.

In soul state, she gains valuable insight from her spirit guide about the rationale that led her to include suffering in her life plan.

Life is a gift, but she does not see it that way. For her, life is a burden. In fact, she views everything as suffering. She must understand the gift that she has been given in this life.

There is nothing like experiencing the worst to bring perspective. A gift is so much easier to appreciate after it has been taken away. Before this life, she was hiding, wasting her time. She was too afraid to move forward, waiting around for all the conditions to be perfect. Life is not like that.

Many lifetimes ago, Angelina formed a belief that she has no value. In that life, at six, she was orphaned when her parents starved to death. Nomadic life was filled with great hardship. Others ignored her as they tended to their own survival, leaving her to forage for her own food. She feared for survival. She remained invisible so that tribal members would not view her as a burden. That life reinforced a belief that she was better alone, that relationships were too dangerous.

At 16, she was taken by a man to bear his children and to care for him. He treated her as property, with the support of tribal members. She had no choice. Ten years later, she went into hiding after she killed him to escape his brutality and servitude. She died decades later having lived an isolated life, struggling to survive.

Even in that life, she had choices. She chose the hard road every time. She chose solitude over communal life. She chose to hide and not to risk connecting with people who she believed only cared about themselves. She came to believe that there was no joy anywhere and that pain was inescapable. No matter what you did, you faced the severity of life.

Angelina learns that these beliefs were replayed and reinforced in many prior lifetimes. Her lack of self-worth remains a *seed that keeps sprouting-up*. By bringing them into her current life, her soul has provided an opportunity for healing and balancing.

To assist, she is gifted with an energetic healing to help release the residue. The release helps her to connect to her divine essence. Sobbing, in the presence of the healing beings, she repeats several times.

I am a divine child of God. God loves me and values me. I have always been loved and valued by him. From this day forward, there will be no doubt that I have value.

After a long embrace, the higher beings depart, and I gently ease her out of trance. Her first words confirm that the session has helped her to see the thread weaving through her past lives to her current life.

> *In the lifetimes in which I was successful, I believed that I had to prove my value. I didn't possess value, I had to earn it. All the lives in which I didn't succeed just reinforced that I didn't have value. In particular, in the lifetime when I was a spiritual leader but couldn't save my followers from persecution, my sense of failure was huge. The pain of that failure has haunted me for centuries.*
>
> *I see the connection to how we live in contemporary society. My current job is 100% about bringing value, the billable hours. You are not valued unless you continue to bring value to the company.*
>
> *It is incredible how freeing it feels to finally reach the basis of my lack of worth.*

The beliefs Angelina's soul held for centuries prompted coping behaviors that fermented pain and robbed her of happiness. To break this long-held pattern of belief and behavior, her soul made a plan that would resurface them. Because they were extreme in their dimension and repetition, their resurfacing was equally extreme.

Through Angelina's regressions and accompanying counseling work, she has released pain and crafted a strategy to overwrite prior falsely held beliefs. She is no longer captive to old beliefs that had trapped her in a cycle of anger and sadness.

She is approaching the work that lies ahead with a new optimism. She is filled with hope and anticipation of the peace and joy that she believes is now within her reach. Practice and patience are her silent helpers.

* * *

In this next case, we meet Jeffrey. His spiritual and emotional growth over the last several years has taught him the important connections between self-acceptance, self-worth, and the capacity for love.

Jeffrey

Jeffrey is 45 years old. He is the oldest of ten siblings born to Mennonite parents. Despite his parents standing in their close-knit religious community, he decided as a young child that this way of life was too restrictive. After graduating high school, he moved from Ohio to Washington D.C. for the opportunities city life held.

He has scheduled a series of transpersonal regressions over the last several years to seek guidance from his guides and his higher self. He is working to overcome what he labels old anxieties and fears. He attributes these to his unforgivable behavior in a past life eons ago and his childhood in this life. He is stuck in his career and has yet to form a long-term relationship with a significant other. He believes both problems are related to his general malaise.

Like many others, his relationship with his parents looms large in his opinion about himself.

> *I wanted to leave the family because I felt that I never fit in and I never could get my father's love or my mother's love back.*

He described his parents' marriage as strained and day-to-day farm life as rigorous. Growing up, Jeffrey was not close to his siblings, who are separated in age by more than 20 years. As an adult, relations have improved with some of them. Most of the family continues to live within the Mennonite community.

Despite the passage of decades, Jeffrey carries beliefs that were shaped during a childhood molded through tragedy and survival. The demands of daily life robbed him of the nurturance he desired.

Jeffrey's family was devasted by a family tragedy. His young cousin died in a fire. For many years, Jeffrey felt responsible, despite his own narrow escape and the fact that he was only 2-years-old at the time.

Decades later, his memory of the fire is palpable.

> *The three of us smelled smoke in the barn, and we went to explore. As we headed into the machine room, there was an explosion that engulfed my older*

cousin. My brother and I ran for help. My mother and aunt came running. My aunt was screaming. I interpreted the screaming as if she was blaming me for the tragedy.

Community members came by over the next several days. No one consoled or comforted me.

I thought people blamed me for the fire.

Jeffrey attributes the fire and his inability to save his cousin as the reason his mother cut-off her love. Despite the trauma, there was no mental health or pastoral counseling provided to family members after the fire.

I lost her love after the fatal fire. She didn't want to go through what my aunt went through when she lost her son in the fire.

Jeffrey experienced a similar lack of emotional nurturance from his father.

I learned that to be loved by my father, I would have to strive. I would have to have value. I had to be good enough.

A year after his first session, Jeffrey returned with less self-loathing. He had taken to heart the counsel received during his first session. Already, he was sensing a positive change within himself. While self-loathing had lessened, it had yet to be replaced with a positive self-worth. With progress, he turned his attention to the general malaise that typifies his life.

I feel like my life is wasted. I don't feel productive as far as helping humanity or doing anything meaningful, including having a child. My law practice is small. It never took off. I am not sure what makes my life meaningful. I think my striving to find something meaningful is related to my always striving to regain my mother's love.

Jeffrey believes that his soul's plan is tied to a past life in which he cut himself off from his soul family because of shame.

I am repeating the same theme, putting myself in the same situation. This time I didn't choose to cut myself off, but my mother and father's lack of love left me feeling completely alone. I feel like I am trying to climb out of a very deep hole.

I am learning the value of love. The one big lesson from this life is that I will never again cut myself off from love. I can see the impact that comes of it. It really messed up my life. I will never do that again.

Somewhat surprised about the change, Jeffrey notes that he has more love in his heart than before.

I have been dating, even though I am not sure it will work out. I feel like I have love for that person.

Sometimes because I feel so bored, I wonder why I am still here. I haven't accomplished my external life goals—having a vibrant practice, helping humanity, having children—that's what makes life worthwhile. I want something that gives meaning to life.

I always believed that if you had love, your life would be fulfilled. I equated being loved with having an external value to humanity.

Jeffrey is trying to break through his earlier belief that his value can be earned.

He is now in the third phase of soul development—learning about love, including love of others and love of self, although he still has beliefs related to the second phase, 'accomplishment and success.' He wonders whether perfecting love is his life purpose.

Once hypnotized, he explores the topic of love with the higher beings who have come to offer their counsel.

You are exploring different types of love, love of others, self-love. The Universe is full of love, there is always love to be found. The love of Source is ever present.

But there is too much junk blocking your experience of love—too many fears and anxieties. They get in the way of your experience of love. You need to stop believing that you have to earn love, and instead accept that you deserve it.

We encourage you to focus on self-acceptance and self-love. You haven't focused on the latter much. You need to feel worthy.

Your worry that personal catastrophe is imminent creates a heavy burden. We have been working with you on this and see that you are ready to release this belief and be more ready to find joy in the moment.

Jeffrey acknowledges to the guides that what he really wants is to feel good about himself. He wants to be happy and content, to allay his fears and to live in the moment. He is assured by the guides that they are working with him to accomplish this.

We want you to feel good, happy, and loved. Just be. Feel the path of love and embrace it. Practice embracing it.

If you choose, the path will open up. *It will come, the Universe will provide it.*

Jeffrey has come to the session requesting that the higher beings help him to release any impediments on his path of wellness, prosperity, and love. He describes a psychic surgery taking place. He senses the removal of old debris that is no longer needed, both beliefs and emotions. He affirms his desire to be more spiritually connected, to embrace the light in whatever he is doing.

They are working on my heart some more. They are telling me to follow the path of love.

Jeffrey recognizes that his strong will is going to be an asset as he works to progress.

In past lives, my ego was so strong it could move mountains. Ego was so prominent. Its dominance was a problem. I am going to give some of this strong will up and turn to Spirit to guide me. I can already sense the energy and freedom of this decision.

The guides have been emphatic that Jeffrey's path to self-worth and self-love require replacing faulty beliefs. On the path to clarity, he has come to understand that he was not singled out for what he experienced as emotional neglect by his mother. He can now recognize that her own emotional state was a factor, including her challenged and trauma-filled relationship with her own father.

I understand that she didn't bond with my other siblings until much later. It wasn't until after the youngest ones were born. I thought I was the only child she didn't love. It was really more complicated.

With my father, he didn't know how to be loving. He didn't have love from his parents. The culture was to be a manly provider, a good upstanding member of the community.

Like most, Jeffrey experienced childhood from the somewhat narrow and singular perspective of a child acutely aware of his own wants and needs. As an adult seeking to heal, he is learning to incorporate a deeper understanding of the complexity of adult life. In particular, he is learning how the demands of raising and providing for ten children on a farm contributed in many ways to what he describes as both his mother and father's emotional detachment.

The guides enumerate his next steps.

Jeffrey still needs to be vigilant. It is still up to him. He has the power, the consciousness, and the will to not allow these thoughts and feelings to creep back. He could revert back, rendering our work for naught.

Jeffrey needs to avoid old fears and anxieties. By dwelling on his perceived lack of parental love, he was giving energy to these fears and anxieties. As a result, his fears and anxieties grew. Only Jeffrey can decide to stop this.

Until new beliefs are fully reinforced, this new way of being isn't solidified. He needs to embrace the feelings they induce and revel in the feeling of love. He is free to be who and what he wants to be. Jeffrey needs to have trust and confidence, knowing that we are here to support him in that effort.

His inability to forgive himself for actions in a past life left him with shame and loathing. Before, his only connection to life was through anger and hate, including anger at Spirit. This left him with nothing to hold onto. All he had was the energy of hatred, anger, self-righteousness, selfishness, and revenge. We have replaced these fragments with light, the energy of universal love.

Jeffrey must embrace the light that he is experiencing here. The more he focuses on it, the more energy will be entrenched in his brain, energy field, and his soul.

You can more easily spread the power and magnitude of light than the energy of darkness. Light is so much easier to grow and spread. Its growth is exponential! When you send out light, it comes back ten-fold.

As the guides prepare to leave, Jeffrey is asked whether he is ready to follow the guidance that they have provided.

Yes. Even if I falter, it would be a travesty not to take advantage of your counsel and the healing you have gifted.

Like all who pursue regression therapy, Jeffrey will need to remain vigilant. His sessions have provided relief, guidance, and a desperately needed emotional boost. He has received help to untangle long held beliefs that caused him to suffer emotionally. But he will need to work to reinforce the clarity that he has gained and the positive feelings that will flow if he can prevent outdated, negative thoughts and worries from creeping back.

His anger and hate have been replaced with a knowing that the more he pursues the path of love, the more his sense of self-worth and self-love will increase.

* * *

In the next case, we meet Siya whose low self-worth has been reinforced through lifetimes of violation, exploitation, and abuse. She learns how her responses to this mistreatment solidified the misery that would become the hallmark of far too many lives.

SIYA

Siya is a 45-year-old single woman who is employed as an executive librarian. She has grown up in a loving and supportive family. She believes that familial love provides an emotional safety net, while romantic love must be earned. She has difficulty forming and asserting an opinion, including speaking-up on her own behalf. Because of this, she has remained silent about her low wages, despite the scope of her responsibility in overseeing a big-city library system.

She was drawn to life between lives hypnotherapy to understand what her soul had planned for this lifetime relative to issues she struggles with. These include low self-worth, excessive weight, and fears preventing her from pursuing romantic relationships.

Over the course of her sessions, Siya would review several past lives that shed light on her current challenges.

Once regressed, Siya revisits a past life in the 1800s. Her name is Daisy, and she became indebted to her older sister Viola who raised her from the age of six after the tragic death of their parents. Siya experiences the loss of her loving parents as abandonment, which seeds fears that grow throughout her lifetime. She believes that no one will love her, and that loving is not worth the risk.

Everyday life is filled with the comforts of upper-class society. But Daisy lives in the shadow of Viola, whose effervescence charms everyone. Her life is filled with obligation, initially caring for Viola's children, and for decades serving as a household servant. Over time, their loving bond is strained as Daisy's unhappiness intensifies over their arrangement. In later life, Daisy reflected on the many years that she spent attending to Viola's needs and solving the problems that she created.

> *I came to believe that I had no intrinsic value, that I had to earn my value. It would have been easier to die and not have to serve Viola.*

Daisy spent a lifetime tolerating Viola's selfishness and dominance. Despite being attracted to Vincent, the butler, she did not pursue a relationship with him, anticipating rejection and fearing that she would incur

Viola's wrath. Her fears were amplified by her unresolved grief for her parents' death. In choosing safety, Daisy retreated from life and in so doing reinforced a belief formed in a lifetime centuries before. In that life, she came to believe that loss of love may be too painful to endure.

Near the end of her life, Daisy reflected back.

I will have to learn to speak up for myself in the future, to have my own voice, and know that just because you speak up for yourself doesn't mean you are being disrespectful. This is connected to self-love.

In soul state, she expresses relief and acquires a deeper understanding of her soul lessons.

I didn't live the life I was meant to live. I was supposed to be more assertive, have a career and a relationship. I had planned to be a teacher. I was meant to be with Vincent. I didn't allow for that relationship to unfold. I was supposed to be more independent. I didn't believe in myself. This is the issue that my soul has been working on. I am going to have to have a do-over life!

I have had many lives in which I was a woman and self-worth was questioned. It is woven into my very fabric.

Delving deep into the past requires that you accept without judgement the barbaric actions levied on millions throughout the course of history. Understanding the impact of prior victimization can do much to free yourself from the grip it may still have on you, despite the passage of centuries. Siya's desire to free herself from debilitating emotions and unproductive coping mechanisms gave her the courage to uncover the origin of the limitations.

Asked if she knows the origin of this theme of self-worth, Siya moves to a lifetime almost a thousand years ago.

Siya describes a life in the 12th century when at age 12, she was literally torn away from her loving parents who were powerless to combat the wealthy lord who kidnapped her. Her name was Misera. She is grossly mistreated. Stripped of her freedom and separated from her loving family, she spent most of her time daydreaming about escaping captivity.

I was caged in a small cell all of the time when I was not serving as his sexual slave. Sex was a horrible ordeal. Food was my only comfort in life. I walled off all my feelings as a way to cope with it. Eight years later, in his presence, I killed myself to escape the torment. I exerted the only control I had, communicating that I would rather end my life than be with him. It took all of my power and strength to escape in this way.

Siya moves beyond the recall of her lives as Daisy and Misera and enters the interlife where she encounters her spirit guide Michael. She is comforted by his loving presence as he guides her to a beautiful beach. She sees herself as a brilliant, bright light.

Michael and she begin a lengthy conversation that initially focuses on her first life in 600 BC in which she died at 8-years old. Her name was Ria. She recalls.

It's weird to be in a human body form. It's like stepping into a pool. You only go a few feet. You can't jump right in. You have to wade in slowly.

Life on earth is difficult, very challenging. Human emotions are deep. They are some of the deepest in the Universe. Sometimes you need a respite.

They discuss other lives that she has had in which she was viewed as property by her husband. She had no voice and assumed limited roles for sex and procreation. The experiences of these lives compounded the feeling of worthlessness experienced during her life as a sexual slave.

Siya becomes more reflective of the issues that have caused her to struggle.

Women are no different than men. We are all the same and deserve to be treated in the same way. People don't treat each other the same out of fear.

I have to learn to respect my own voice and know that it has worth. This will be the focus of my next lifetime. I have opinions, but I don't think that others will value my opinion. I want others to want to hear what I have to say. I can achieve that without being in a powerful external position.

Michael's loving assurances provide comfort and insight.

Siya will need to learn to trust herself, to trust that whatever unfolds will be positive and benefit her. She needs to apply her strength. Good things will happen as long as she believes that they can happen. When you don't believe that good things can happen, you close the door to their unfolding. Siya has closed the door to many things in her life. Developing confidence is a big part of what she still needs to work on.

Siya understands that she will need to employ all of her strength to overcome deeply embedded feelings of unworthiness.

The topic of the conversation shifts to Siya's struggle with weight.

In her lifetime as Misera in the 12th century, she was entrapped by the ruler who was captivated by her extreme beauty. Beauty had become a liability. Siya's weight has become a disguise, protecting her from the type of victimization that she experienced in that lifetime. Weight obscures her beauty. But it also reinforces the belief that she is not good enough or attractive enough. So, it further eats away at her self-worth.

She has to reconcile that beauty is not reflected in your size. Self-worth does not come from your size. It comes from loving yourself despite what size you are. It's an example of how she is not leaving the door open to have other people value her, because she is not valuing herself. The biggest obstacle that is keeping love out of her life is her disbelief. Once she comes to fully understand this, love will come, regardless of her weight.

Misera, Daisy, Ria, and Siya all had been loved and cherished by their parents. But repeated mistreatment by men left Siya fearing equating sex and love.

Sex was polluted in her prior experiences. It was not something from which she could garner pleasure. She believes that sex can be repulsive. Siya is not in tune with her sexuality because of this belief.

She believes that when someone is interested in you, all they want is sex. So, relationships have been something that she has chosen to avoid.

All of this is an effort to self-protect. She fears intimacy. She is protecting herself from rejection, protecting herself from abandonment, and protecting herself from becoming a sexual commodity.

At a deep level, she believes that the joy of love is not worth the risk of losing it or experiencing the pain.

The path forward begins to surface.

Siya has to become comfortable in herself as a sexual being. It is not something to fear. She needs to let go of her inhibitions. They are holding her back. She needs to live life.

Her desire to be more independent is intertwined with her intention to overcome her inhibitions. It is unfolding even though it has been a slower process then was hoped. She is on the road to doing what she needs to do. She needs to be patient in this knowing and accept that everything happens at the right time and right place.

She needs to learn that it is okay to take risks. It's okay to be vulnerable. Opening one's heart is worth the risk. She needs not to run away from love. Being scared is part of it, she just can't let herself be overwhelmed by it.

As the session begins to draw to a close, Michael and the members of Siya's council are quick to offer their praise.

She has embraced the plan she set in place for this lifetime. It's all positive. She chose a professional career that has enabled independence. She is finding her voice and building confidence that her opinions will be valued. She has been open to grow, fully embracing the journey.

She is growing better able to accept that she is worthy of love.

She is a good soul with very good energy. She should carry that forward because it will take her far, farther than she can imagine.

The best is yet to come, much lies ahead for her. She will reach a point in which she will revel in the joys of life. She has been through a lot in previous lives. Life is meant to be rewarding for her this time.

The closing words of the session not only speak to Siya but resonate for all.

Humans come to understand many things through their physical senses, but not love. Love is an energy. Soul energy is love. That's what we are at the core. Most humans don't understand this. They get lost in the murk of earthly existence, which obscures the true meaning of love. If they loved themselves truly and freely, they would not get confused. So, if you are able to stay true to yourself, you will be able to find love.

When you quiet your mind and still your body, the energy that is pulsating through you is love. You can't quantify it. That is why people who meditate have so much peace, because in meditation, you experience love. That's what is running through the body.

God, the Source, is the same energy that is pulsing through our veins. It is the same energy that leaves the body and continues on after it is shed at death and our soul goes back to the Source. It is not something that you can see or quantify.

The Source is a significantly larger manifestation of this energy, larger than the Universe. You have heard many times that each soul is like a drop of water in the vastness of the oceans. God is the ocean, and each soul is like a drop of that water. It is the same energy. God is infinite love energy.

In your successive human lives, you are trying to understand love to the best of your abilities. You are trying to live in that love so that it is all you exude to those around you. When you reach that point, your experience of life changes dramatically.

Humans are trying to remember the part of themselves that is just love. They are seeking to live and bask in love. Those who allow love to guide them pave the way for it to usher in peace and bliss that awaits.

For Tina, Eleanor, Angelina, Jeffrey, and Siya, love is the energy that is now mending their fractured self-worth and fueling their emotional healing and spiritual growth.

An empty lantern provides no light.
Self-care is the fuel that allows your light to shine brightly.

—UNKNOWN

7

SELF-CARE

Many reach a point in life when they realize that they rarely, if ever, prioritize their own needs. For some, it may be a habit formed over years or lifetimes ago. Often, this realization comes after discovering that *they can no longer run on empty.*

Caring for yourself is not a selfish act. It is an indication that you have begun to balance compassion for others with compassion for yourself. Accomplishing this requires that you are on your list of priorities, preferably near the top.

Taking care of yourself necessitates that you have established personal boundaries and that *no* is not only in your vocabulary, but you are able to utter it when appropriate.

Does caring for yourself leave you feeling guilty? Does this guilt lead you to meet the need of others before you take care of yourself? If so, you must realize that you can't sacrifice yourself for other people just because you love them. Even sacrifice has its limits. You must learn to resist allowing others to be your priority, while allowing yourself to be an option.

If you have done so for a prolonged period, there is a cost. The price is not only paid in time, energy, and other resources, but it may have cost you your health and wellbeing. In extreme cases, the cost of not caring for yourself can be your life.

Being dutiful and responsible are positive qualities. But in excess, they preclude balance, a necessary achievement for the soul.

* * *

The five cases that follow illustrate how important self-care is to one's physical and emotional well-being. Each of them is also a reminder that balance is foundational to the soul's spiritual growth and advancement.

JASMINE

Jasmine is a 55-year-old senior manager at a Fortune 500 company where she began her career as an entry level clerk. Her drive and determination fueled her professional advancement and success, but all that has now evaporated. She described herself as resilient and happy-go-lucky, until the last several months.

> *I feel burned out, stuck, and depressed. I am not bouncing back like I used to. I'm disappointed with where my life is right now, and I don't know how to fix it. The future looks empty and bleak.*

The situation between Jasmine and her partner of twenty years is also strained.

> *Our relationship is stuck. It feels suffocating. It is neither empowering nor enabling. I am mindful that as I get older, I need more alone time. Unfortunately, given my partner's reaction, I feel guilty wanting to be alone. So, I don't get enough alone time.*

Jasmine scheduled a regression session, seeking insight about getting life back on track.

Often, people experience one life during a past life regression, less frequently; people hop from one lifetime to another. When this happens, the guides are showing the person that a pattern has been set in place and reinforced during different lifetimes. This was the case for Jasmine.

Jasmine first revisits a lifetime in the heartland living on a farm with her parents and male siblings during the late 1860's. She is 10-years-old. Her name is Elba. Her father and four older brothers are rarely home, given the demands of working the fields. As the only girl in the family, she is expected to help her mother maintain the household. She is responsible for cooking and taking care of household chores as well as feeding the chickens and cows. She does not attend school and doesn't read, but she is inquisitive.

I would rather be out exploring things. I am very curious. I get scolded for daydreaming and not paying attention. I am smart, but it is not very useful in this life. I'm bored, so I go outside to escape. I get in trouble when I get back.

My mother works very hard and is always tired. So, I feel guilty when I sneak outside to explore and go off by myself.

I'm envious of my dad and brothers. I would rather be out doing the farm work. The housework is boring and hard work. And when they are gone, it's lonely.

Jasmine moves to another life as a 23-year-old man, his name is Edgar. It is 1922. He lives alone in New York City, having grown up in the country in a large family with several younger sisters and older brother.

I needed to get away. I didn't really fit in. My family was so traditional, and the farming just didn't suit me. I felt like there was more to life. My family was not happy about that. They wanted me to stay, but I had to get away. It was a burden for my siblings to keep the farm going and to care for mom and dad. But I just had to do it. I had to see what was out in the world, to see if I could survive in the city. It took courage for me to uproot and move. I felt guilty about it.

Life in the city is scary and hard. I can't afford much, a tiny little place. But there is hope for doing better here. I am doing research and writing for a lawyer.

I have hope for the future.

Jasmine moves to another point in Edgar's life. He is now in his late 30s and married with two children, a 10-year-old daughter and a 15-year-old son. The global depression has disrupted life for Edgar and his family.

I work all the time. Even with my promotion, I barely make enough to feed my family, so my wife has to do laundry for other families to make money to make ends meet. I know it could be a lot worse. So many neighbors lost their jobs, lost everything. There are so many homeless and hungry people. I feel sorry for them.

My plans to buy a house, get more education, and open my own business had to be shelved because of the stock market crash. My dreams were not realized. It's disappointing and depressing, but I don't see a way out.

We move ahead two decades. Edgar is in his 50s and has returned to the family farm. He realizes that he fared better financially as he compares his situation to that of his birth family. Although he didn't become a lawyer, his son is pursuing a law degree with his financial support. The trip home prompts reflection.

From the perspective of the higher self, we come to understand characteristics of the eternal nature of Jasmine's prior selves.

I was adventurous and curious, never satisfied with what I had in Edgar's life. I always wanted to try something different.

I was just like Elba!

I chose to be a man in that life to compare the differences between being a woman and a man, to explore the impact that gender would have. There are advantages to being a man. It was obvious with the schooling of Edgar's children that more was expected of his son than of his daughter. The type of work offered is another example. Women have to work harder.

I let the culture define me. The people I worked with expected tradition. I went along and didn't do anything to rock the boat. I was too afraid. I think I had many lives in which I was afraid to buck the dominant culture, even though I saw that it was wrong. I wanted to fit in.

On the one hand, I am curious and adventurous, and I want to go out and try something new, but then I reach a point where I am afraid to do more.

Looking back on Edgar's life, I'm disappointed that I didn't do anything more creative in my lifetime. I regret that I didn't try new things.

In leading Jasmine back to Edgar and Elba's lives, Jasmine's guide placed a spotlight on the beliefs that have been fueling her emotions and behaviors in lifetimes that straddled two millennia.

Jasmine struggles between doing what's best for herself and others. She views kindness and compassion in conflict with meeting her own needs and desires. It's a constant struggle. There is a way to balance the two. She needs to include herself as a priority. There is no reason for her to be afraid. She has demonstrated that she does not need to conform.

With this insight in hand, Jasmine is more receptive to the counsel of her guide and higher self about how to balance competing desires.

Until recently, Jasmine has been happy in a same sex union for twenty years, long before such a choice was socially acceptable. She chose to defy convention and not have children. In her career, she excelled in a male dominated environment. Each of these demonstrate she was not limited by her fears. Her beliefs of conforming didn't hold her back.

Jasmine acknowledges that she has shown courage before, so she should be able to do it again.

I think that this is something that I might be ready to do. I just need the courage to take the risks to make it happen.

I don't need to feel guilty for taking time for myself and caring for myself. Twenty years ago, I started writing a play, but I never finished it. One of my colleagues keeps encouraging me to take the time to finish the play and write the book I have been dreaming about.

I have allowed too many things and people to become obstacles. There are so many demands. If I choose to prioritize myself, I feel that others will be disappointed. I keep thinking that I should take a sabbatical, go someplace by myself and write, but I haven't.

Jasmine has realized that it is her own beliefs that have held her back.

There's nothing wrong with needing alone time. It's normal. It's not a matter of conforming. My responsibilities are sucking me dry, taking my time up. The people in my life will have to understand.

Jasmine's guide has provided inspiration that led Jasmine to uncover the beliefs that were limiting her. In doing so, they have pointed the way to breaking stifling patterns that had repeated lifetime after lifetime. Her guides' encouraging words offer a new rallying cry.

Let nothing stop you.

Old patterns have been replaced with freedom. Confusion replaced with clarity about the choices that are hers to make. In the process of revisiting two past lives, she has learned how important it will be to balance the needs of others with her own needs and desires. For Jasmine, self-care is no longer an option. It is the key to the happiness that she desperately wants. In the future, self-care is paramount.

* * *

In the next case, we meet Lily. Learning to care for herself is not only a priority, but it essential for her survival.

LILY

Lily is a 34-year-old project manager, employed by a defense contractor. She suffers from sleep disorders. She is divorced after a decade long marriage to her high school sweetheart, whom she still loves but can no longer live with due to his serious mental health issues. Since her divorce, Lily has been actively dating and hopes that she would find a lifelong partner.

Lily pursed regression therapy hoping to better understand her soul's purpose and plan for this lifetime. After several past life regressions over the course of five years, she scheduled a life between lives session. She was particularly interested in gaining insight about her pattern of interpersonal relationships, including the ups and downs of her dating life.

Once hypnotized, Lily easily reports from the vantage point within her mother's womb, that she is excited about the upcoming incarnation but a little nervous. She knows that she has embedded surrender, peace, and self-care and love into her soul's plan. This is the first time that she planned to focus on self-care and self-love, exhausted by many previous lifetimes that were focused on service to others.

I need a break. My chronic fatigue will make it difficult for me to serve other people. I will be more easily worn out and have to use my energy for myself. I only brought 40% of my energy into this life. Another 40% of my energy will incarnate elsewhere so that I might have the experience of being taken care of.

Moving back in time, Lily briefly visits a past life in which she died relatively young. Floating out of her body, she moves through a brilliant, blue liquid light that morphs to purple.

Having arrived in the afterlife, she has an emotional reunion with a past love. They have shared many lifetimes together. He apologizes for again having left her broken hearted so that he could work on becoming more self-confident and independent.

I am supposed to be focusing on self-care, so each time he leaves provides space for me to do so. But neither one of us expected it to be so difficult. That's why I decided to die so young in that past life. Even though it was an aspect of our respective soul plans that I had agreed to, when he left, it was too painful and lonely. I was stuck in grief.

Lily's spirit guide Scion joins her and escorts her to a large gathering of family and friends. She is fortified by the warmth of their welcome and love. After this reception, Scion draws her attention to some of the more important aspects of her soul's plan.

You are supposed to keep yourself energetically charged by doing things that give you joy. There needs to be balance in your life, between these joys and supporting yourself financially. In addition to serious matters, focus on fun and hobbies that interest you. The stability that your career provides is meant to be the foundation so that you have time for joy.

If something is not serving you, let it go. Don't hold onto things that do not serve you. Your tendency to put others first causes stress. Taking care of everyone else leaves you drained.

You have built many things into your plan to help you to focus on yourself. You dread some of these because they move you out of your comfort zone.

Your soul group is collectively working on self-love, balance, relationships, spirituality, and charity. Through your many lives, you have developed empathy and compassion for others, but in this life, you have chosen to develop compassion for yourself.

The extreme challenges created by your husband's mental illness was a catalyst for your exploration of boundary setting. Setting boundaries is totally new for you. Even after the divorce, he kept pushing you to learn to take care of yourself. You have had a long history of prioritizing the needs of others. Hopefully, this insight will help you begin to focus on self-care.

You have learned to love yourself, but you overfocus on serving others. You have not yet achieved a balance, but you can learn how to. Your friend Sam is an example for you to follow.

You built distance into your romantic relationships as part of your soul planning process. You wanted to make progress on self-care, and you didn't want to get weighed down or distracted. You wanted to avoid slipping into the caretaker role. You were not looking for nurturance by others, you wanted to learn to care for yourself.

In order to have the long-term relationship that you desire, you need to remain focused on self-care. Past relationships were intended to be temporary as part of your learning process. You need to be your number one priority, even within a relationship.

Your purpose in this lifetime is self-care and self-love. You have to be energized to be able to help others. Your highest goal is to surrender to your own plan. It is a necessity. Your past choices left you exhausted and drained.

The scene shifts as Scion escorts Lily to meet with the members of her council. The space has a serious, formal ambiance. There she is greeted by a group of seven.

The council members echo what Scion has already told Lily.

You are a leader in your soul group. You have more experience than the other group members in terms of service and giving to others. Because you are so driven and take on responsibility easily, you have trouble balancing your own needs.

For several minutes, they share their perspective on her manifesting the highest version of herself.

> *We see that you have lots of energy and can use it to stay healthy. You will be very good at taking care of yourself when you focus on this. Setting clear boundaries will protect your energy. Move out of your comfort zone to expand your peace and joy. You will have to develop routines that are built on self-care that overcome your tendency to procrastinate.*

Lily acknowledges to council members that she has reservations about her capacity to realize this highest version of herself. She is afraid and is not convinced that making the effort will reap the desired results. Her honesty has underscored yet another impediment that is standing in her way.

Lily's honesty is met with acceptance and honesty by council members.

> *Many souls would get discouraged by the challenge you have taken on for yourself. You are doing well. We have seen what you have accomplished. You have our full confidence. We believe in you. We love you and are very proud of you.*

The feedback and guidance that Lily received from both her spirit guide and council members answered the questions that led her to past life and life between lives hypnotherapy. Their unconditional acceptance provided needed encouragement. The experience will serve to motivate her as she begins the hard work to learn to prioritize self-care.

Self-care is something you must learn and ultimately master. For those responsible for employees, congregants, partners, children, infirmed or otherwise incapacitated loved ones, prioritizing self over another is a challenge. Many struggle to strike the right balance.

While sacrificing oneself for the sake of others may be viewed as the responsible or even heroic thing to do, it comes at a cost to the soul who must bring balance to every aspect of its eternal character and experience. Lily's long journey to self-care can be a wake-up call for those who are just realizing that they too deserve the time, energy, care, and devotion that they so willingly and easily give to others.

* * *

In the next instance, we are introduced to Esther. Her difficulty striking a balance between self-care and care of others brought her to the brink of death. In the process, she learned invaluable lessons about the human need to exert control over our lives.

Esther

Esther is a 58-year-old retiree who left her job several years ago to care for her elderly parents after a decades long career in information technology. She is close to two of her three siblings. During the intake interview, it was apparent that despite loving parents, her childhood was filled with trauma, including her mother's serious mental illness and the sexual assault of her brother by an extended family member.

Esther suffers from migraines, chronic fatigue, debilitating anxiety, and is unable to swallow medicine. She scheduled a past life regression with hopes of gaining understanding that might lead to the elimination of physical ailments.

Rather than the planned journey to a past life, Esther initially finds herself peering back in her current life at age four. As she moves deeper into trance, she is joined by her spirit guide.

She is alone outside in the dark. She is crying because her brother Mathew told her about the bad things that happened to him. This prompts Esther's recall of her own sexual victimization by the same uncle.

My uncle's here. He's doing things he shouldn't do. I see it. I am sitting on his lap.

Sobbing, she hears herself yell out.

Leave me alone. I don't like it when you put me on your lap. Adults probably wouldn't let you do that. You only like little kids because they won't say anything.

With more intense emotion, Esther cries.

Nanny, where are you?

Why is this happening? I don't like him. He's creepy. Why is he always putting me on his lap when I come to nanny's house? I'm cute, but it is not my fault. Nanny used to yell at my uncle and tell him he was bad.

But maybe she didn't know what he was doing to me. I never said anything.

Why are the people I love doing such a bad job protecting me? Don't they love me?

Anguished, Esther repeats.

I love my nanny.

The scene shifts, and Esther sees herself running to her grandmother. They embrace. She is telling me that she will take care of me. She senses that Mathew has joined her, and they both are wrapped in the love and safety of their grandmother's arms.

In a state of expanded awareness induced through hypnotic trance, Esther recognizes the presence of the higher beings who have joined her to enable release and healing.

Esther agrees to allow the soul of her abusive uncle to be called into the scene. He enters but remains several feet away as she and Mathew remain nestled in their grandmother's protective embrace.

He is saying he was sick. He's repeating it over and over again. He is hoping for forgiveness.

Somewhat tepidly, Ester says she can forgive him. She remains calm for several minutes before remembering a different, recurring childhood scene.

They are making me eat the food. I don't want to eat. I am going to throw up. I feel like that lots of times. I throw up on the kitchen table. I can't hide it anymore. I won't do it anymore.

Everybody's trying to control me all the time. I won't let them. I am in control. I will decide what to eat!

Even though more than 50 years have passed, Esther has not been able to reconcile the lack of protection with the belief that her nanny and parents loved her. This confusion has been made worse by her tendency to care for others—serving others has become a means for earning love.

Esther's attention shifts to events surrounding her near-death last year. Already divorced, with her brothers living across the country, and soon after the death of her parents, Esther found herself alone with no one to care for her.

Nobody was there to help me. Nobody was there to protect me.

I was really sick. They couldn't figure it out. I was failing. I almost died because I wouldn't take the medicine.

It was a test.

I'm all alone. Nobody was helping me. I don't have a husband to take care of me. I was afraid that I would be all alone if something happened to me.

Maybe I wanted to die. But I can't die because I am not finished helping people. I have so much to do. If I die, there is too much left undone. I have to help a lot of people. So, I have to be here. I have to stay. My brothers need me.

Eventually, my brothers came. They showed me that they love me. They saved me. When I felt my brother's love, I decided to stay.

It's a sort of tug of war. I want to be with them all the time, but they are far away. I feel good when I am helping them. I love helping them. I always feel better when I am helping people.

After a torturous review of these painful episodes, Esther is willing to speak to her spirit guide. A bright, calming light fills the space as Claudia enters Esther's awareness. She speaks first about Esther's plan for this lifetime.

Esther chose her family to be of service to them. She always likes to help. She was prepared for the challenges and trauma that unfolded because she is so strong. But this led her to hide her own pain. They all believed that she was fine. She hid her suffering and sadness.

Given her mistreatment as a child, Esther confused love, protection, and service. She could not understand how those who loved her could not protect her and her brother.

Swallowing food as a child, and medicine as an adult, has been Esther's way of exerting control over situations in which she did not feel in control. She could control life and death—swallow or not swallow. Swallowing is a symbol of the control that she exerts over her own life. It was her way of declaring that she was valuable and in control, even when the adults were not taking charge to protect her as they should have.

Esther equates love with service. So alone, with no one to help her, she concluded she was unloved. She had lost her desire to live.

Going forward, she will need to reconcile the conflicting emotions that decades ago entangled love, protection, and service. To achieve this, she will need to release the past.

Claudia helped Esther to understand the power that she has. Something she herself had not consciously recognized, despite being able to exert it.

She was ready to die because the burden of this life of service was so great. In her desperation, she saw death as the only way to reach a place of peace.

She now understands that even loved ones can make grave mistakes. She can accept that even with their imperfections, their love is reciprocal.

Even though they did a bad job protecting me, that doesn't mean that they didn't love me.

Surfacing painful memories and confusion, she is able to decide whether she will free herself from the bondage of those memories. She alone has the power to release the memories. She alone has the power to forgive them and free herself from the burden of carrying the pain.

Esther's higher self offers further thoughts on how to move beyond the sadness of the past.

The intention is to learn to balance service with self-care. Self-care is essential.

Esther needs to allow herself to be happy. She needs to prioritize herself and her own happiness. She needs to do more of the things that make her feel good. She needs to take more time for rest.

The move to Florida will give her more time for relaxation. There will be more time for fun, to golf and garden. It will be good for her to find a nice, loving companion to spend time with.

Esther admits that it will take practice to break her pattern of gravitating to people who need her and who do not reciprocate. But she is heartened by the counsel and encouragement that she has received. As her sessions draw to an end, she affirms her determination to take better care of herself.

I can do it. This is my time for joy, happiness, and love.

Breaking long standing patterns of behavior is not easy. Motivation is a driving force. Your success increases when your desire for change is coupled with an understanding of the beliefs and emotions that have fueled unsatisfying patterns.

Esther chose life. And then, she chose to live in a manner that would fortify rather than continue to drain her. She came to understand the origin of her limiting beliefs. In doing so, she freed herself from painful truths of her past. The support she received from her guide and higher self sparked a commitment to balance serving others with self-care. Honoring this vow will yield the joy, love, and happiness that she desires.

* * *

We next meet Martina who, like Esther, has difficulty striking a balance between self-care and care of others. Her soul drew attention to this through a series of serious health scares. In the process, Martina learns the importance of bringing balance and establishing personal boundaries.

MARTINA

Martina is a 55-year-old grandmother who recently relocated near her son's family to be closer to her first grandchild. The onset of cancer more than a decade ago accelerated her spiritual journey and a self-healing regimen. She has recovered twice from cancer but recently was diagnosed with a third.

Despite its recurrence, she remains very positive about the disease and what it has to offer her. She is self-confident and blessed with a strong sense of personal power.

> *I have never been terrified, upset, or depressed about the disease. I have viewed it as a wake-up call. I call the cancer my teacher, and I want to understand what I am supposed to learn from it. I don't view it as my enemy. It is telling me that I need to go deeper into myself.*

Martina believes in a creator, an original source of life, but has rejected the rigid structure of her religion of birth. Her rejection of organized religion is counter balanced by a deep spirituality.

> *I continue to have to walk my own path. This route may be more difficult, but I believe it is my job to look inward for the answers. I know there are higher beings who I can ask for help, but at the end of the day, I must assume responsibility for myself. With knowledge, understanding, acceptance, and work, I can achieve what is labeled a miracle.*

The process of healing that Martina began in 2007 has been filled with many lessons and much growth. Like the Chinese symbol for crisis, which is identical to the symbol for opportunity, the crisis of cancer provided Martina with the opening to focus on herself.

Martina liberated herself from decades of cultural conditioning. By her own description, the growth has been dramatic, including learning to prioritize herself and to establish personal boundaries.

I've learned to understand and accept that I need to make myself a priority. I know that I deserve my own love and other people's love, and that I need to take care of myself. For many years, it was difficult to accept gifts, including gifts of kindness. I now know the importance of receiving.

My concept of God has expanded in the process. I now experience my own divinity. I know that we are all one.

Despite tremendous growth, Martina understands that there is more insight to be gained. Her hope is that she will come to understand what else her cancer hopes to teach her through regression work.

Encouraged by a lifelong friend who values the healing and wisdom of past life regression, she scheduled a session. Once in trance, Martina finds herself in Paris. It's 1894. She is overlooking the plaza in front of Notre Dame Cathedral. She gasps when she sees a man that she knew in the past, although she is uncertain of their relationship. She cries, overcome with emotion.

Martina's past life review is placed on hold as her focus shifts to her home in Miami and the spirit of a young man who she often sees in her garden. He identifies himself as Mark. He has attached himself to Martina. He had been looking for her since their life together in Paris and finally found her. He is confused, not realizing that he is dead. He has remained at the plaza in front of Notre Dame where he used to sell his vegetables. He loves the cathedral and is upset about the destruction caused by the massive fire in the spring of 2019.

The scene shifts back to the garden, and Martina finds herself looking directly at Mark. She notices that he has relaxed, he is less anxious. He tells her that he misses her.

He has been attracted to her life force, but he realizes that he must move on. To help, beings from the higher realms arrive to escort Mark into the interlife. Martina whispers good-bye.

The scene Martina experiences shifts again, and we are joined by Paul, a higher being. He has come to help Martina understand and provide insight regarding her cancer.

The cancer that has sickened Martina is not coming from within. It is coming from outside of her. Discarnate spirits are attracted to her energy. It's as if they are plugging in to recharge. It is depleting her energy and weakening her ability to fight illness.

The cancer is not what people think. The ones who fear it are wrong. The cancer is not what kills them. They experience death because they don't understand. One day, humanity will understand that there is no death.

Martina cannot help everyone. It is not selfish to not help. She has to learn to set boundaries.

Martina is healthy. She can keep on living. She should not worry about whether she has cancer. The cancer can dwell within Martina. It's okay. It's not robbing her of joy.

People around her worry. They interfere. There are many, many, many people around her all of the time. If you can imagine the nucleus of a cell with many hairs attached, you will understand what it is like for her. These people are very tiring. It's not a matter of having more time by herself. They are still attached even in her alone time.

It's her job to stand like a tree full of limbs, full of leaves. It's a beautiful thing. She is transmuting their worry in the same way that a tree breathes out oxygen from the carbon dioxide it has taken in. She's learning to become a tree, to heal others. But Martina cannot help everyone.

As Paul prepares to depart, he repeats.

It is not selfish to not help. She has to learn to set boundaries.

Once Paul departs, a healing session ensues. The healing beings who have joined spend minutes infusing Martina with healing energy and light. She is comforted and energized in their healing embrace. Several minutes later, I bring her up from the trance. In the counseling session that follows, Martina acknowledges the scale of the task ahead.

I could feel tons of beings and people attached to me. It was overwhelming.

We discussed a way forward that emphasizes the balance of care of others and care of self.

I have to learn to protect my energy. There are many who are taking my energy. I still need to find the right balance.

Although Martina's soul agreed to help others by becoming the metaphorical tree, it is essential that she set an intention that her own energy not be depleted.

In order to remain healthy, as well as emotionally grounded, she needs a minimum amount of energy. There is no intent for her to sacrifice health, peace, or joy in order to help others. Loving herself means recognizing and honoring her own needs.

As Paul was quick to remind her, she cannot help everyone. Having appropriate boundaries is not selfish. Self-care is essential for survival.

* * *

In the next case, we are introduced to Roberta, who is learning similar lessons. She has much compassion for others but has yet to prioritize care of herself.

ROBERTA

Roberta is a 60-year-old, married psychiatric social worker who finds her work enjoyable but all-consuming and draining.

Despite appearances to the contrary, Roberta's birth family was extremely *troubled.* Her abusive father's long-standing addiction and her mother's detachment reflected the pain of their own childhoods. In both instances, their childhood was marred by chronic addiction, mental illness, domestic violence, and the murder of her paternal grandmother by her husband. A bright star in Roberta's otherwise sad childhood was the birth of her younger sister and close friend Regina.

Roberta was kicked out of her home at 16 and married a year later. She put her husband through school and supported him for the next 15 years before he abandoned her and their two children.

A later marriage to someone who was already financially secure did not change this dynamic. Roberta remained the family provider. A millionaire in his own right, her new husband began to hide his money in case they would later divorce. For a second time, she found herself with a partner who wanted a nurturing caretaker as a wife.

Roberta has a loving and richly rewarding relationship with her eldest daughter but a strained relationship with her youngest daughter. From her earliest days, her youngest daughter would proclaim that she hated her mom. At 14, she ran away. Now with five children of her own, she struggles with a serious addiction. She and her children rely on Roberta for financial support.

Exhausted from endless 12-hour workdays, Roberta is exasperated that there is never enough and that she has spent much of her life paying for the mistakes that others have made.

Like many others who have scheduled a life between lives session, Roberta hoped to better understand her life in a way that would guide future decisions and actions.

She would learn much from her guide Edizir who was happy to offer his counsel.

> *Roberta believes that she must carry others who are not fulfilling their obligations.*
>
> *Even though she has fulfilled her life goals and exceeded her own expectations, she is driven by a view that there is always one more thing that she can do. She tries too hard. This contributes to her sense that she is persevering alone in this life.*
>
> *Her life is tipped in favor of accepting others' responsibilities. She needs to understand that what she has done already is enough. She has met her obligations as well as the obligations of the others. By habit, she is paying-off the debts of others.*
>
> *She can live without rescuing everyone.*
>
> *To live without pain, Roberta needs to bring balance into her life.*
>
> *Life is not only for obligation. Joy is as necessary as duty! Duty should be combined with joy. When you are performing a duty, it should be done with joy and spoken about with joy and rewarded with joy.*

Everyone knows someone like Roberta. In fact, if they are honest, most love people like Roberta who are super responsible and dependable. They may be a favorite person for that very reason. That person will always say 'yes,' regardless of the imposition or how big a favor you ask of them. Yes, is the answer even when it will cost them in time, money, or energy.

Edizir gave Roberta sound advice, which serves as a gift to all those who have trouble setting boundaries.

NO can be the best answer when a loved one struggling with addiction asks to borrow money that you know will never be returned and will likely fuel their habit. *NO* can be the best answer when your teenager, who has yet to assume any responsibilities, begs you to buy her a car. *NO* can be the best answer for the lover who asks to come back into your life after leaving you for a third time to be with yet another *someone else*.

The list is quite long of situations for which *no* can be the best answer. Not only is *no* likely in the long-term best interest of the other, but being able to say no, to set boundaries and to honor them, is an indication of your self-respect.

If Roberta is able to implement Edizir's advice, the boundaries she establishes will help her loved ones assume greater responsibility for themselves. Most importantly, she will find that she is less often exhausted or exasperated.

There are complicated reasons why so many are challenged to set reasonable boundaries. Regardless of the underlying need, breaking this emotionally and physically costly pattern is the first important step. Even when such behavior is motivated by compassion, this too must be balanced in the process of spiritual growth.

* * *

In this final case, we meet Carla, who, like Roberta and Lily, has boundless compassion for loved ones. And like both of them, the emotional and physical cost has become too high.

Carla

Carla is a 54-year-old highly educated, corporate executive whose work has led to international deployments. She is strong, driven, and determined, and in her own words—a force of nature.

She assumes primary decision making and holds medical and financial power-of-attorney for both of her 90-year-old divorced parents, who reside in their separate homes with the support of 24 hour-a-day, in-home care. The logistics of the arrangement are encumbered by her parents living in a state more than 2000 miles away from her own home.

The geographical distance is just one of the myriad challenges that Carla copes with. Although she has two siblings, one of whom lives near their parents, she almost singlehandedly carries the responsibility for their care.

> *I believe I must do everything humanly possible that is within my power and abilities to meet the needs of those I love.*

The strain of her parental caretaking responsibilities has been exacerbated by her siblings and husband's lack of support. Additionally, almost a decade ago, a beloved soul intimate, her only emotional support, died.

The culmination of these stressors and disappointments initially led her to regression therapy and spiritual counseling. She believed at the deepest level that guidance from the higher realms would help her to cope.

In a first past life, Carla revisited an ancient life in which she was powerless to protect and defend herself. Upon venturing into a foreign village, she was imprisoned and ultimately killed because she was different from the villagers. She is aware that in her current lifetime, she has used her personal and professional power to right perceived wrongs of others who were too vulnerable to protect themselves.

After initial counseling and past life regressions, Carla scheduled an LBL, hoping to gain a clearer sense of her life purpose and to better understand key relationships. Additionally, she hoped to find a way out of the searing emotional pain that has characterized her life during the last decade.

Reaching trance depth, she easily reports from her vantage point within the womb. When asked about her upcoming life, she begins crying uncontrollably and says that it is going to be very hard.

> *I'm not sure I want to do it. I just have to do it and get it over with. It's just something I have to do.*

Carla is not easily consoled but has no plans to turn back. She is determined to find the peace and understanding that she believes she will find in the journey to the interlife.

I can't keep living the way I am living.

After she calms, we resume movement. She reaches the afterlife and is welcomed by a bevy of loving beings, including her soul intimate who died a decade before.

I was the only one she would accept love from. It's scary for her, but she trusted me. She understands the power of love, but she only knows how to give it. She doesn't receive it from anyone but me. I would be happy if she learned to receive love from others. I want her to be happy. That's what she deserves, but I like being the one she loves the most.

For Carla, learning to care for herself is a preface to letting others care for her.

Carla's spirit guide Thomas joins us, and the conversation shifts to the questions that she has raised for the LBL.

Endurance is a theme of Carla's lifetime. She hoped to build her strength and to remind herself how brave she is. Things hurt her deeply. She is trying to learn to balance vulnerability with bravery and strength. This lifetime is serving as a test for her. She's only recently begun training. She is preparing to teach others.

Her immediate family brings her pain, yet she chooses to help them anyway. They are very difficult people, yet she selected them as she made her life plan. These souls do not appreciate what she does for them.

She must decide at what point do you continue to serve and help? And at what price? But making those decisions is so difficult because it is easier for her to not be loved than to be loved. Love is painful for her because of what has happened in earlier lives.

Her experience of joy is limited because she is stuck in the familiarity of the pain. To break this pattern, she will need to experience new love. This most likely will not happen within her marriage. Even the thought of this possibility is threatening to her. She believes that once she makes a commitment, she must honor it.

Thomas' description of Carla's marital situation illustrates the challenge that she faces trying to balance care and love for herself with care and love of others.

In the exchange with Thomas, Carla's higher self notes that she deserves to be happy. She acknowledges that she is ready to make some of the changes that need to be made in order to have more joy and less pain. But it is clear that her beliefs are leaving her conflicted and unsatisfied.

Carla needs to be willing to let others be hurt. It's hard to do, but sometimes it's necessary for their growth.

She has to accept that it could be for everyone's benefit, not just her own.

Thomas' counsel is threatening and prompts Carla to come back out of the trance. I begin again to help her relax and reenter trance. Beings from the angelic realm reappear to calm her, so she can decide whether to proceed. After several minutes, she becomes aware that her guide Thomas has returned.

Carla is on her path. It's difficult, but she is learning what she came to learn. There is more for her to learn that will test her strength. She must learn to balance her vulnerability with her strength, including with those for whom she accepts responsibility. These relationships potentially offer mutual benefit.

Her relationship with her father is just one example.

Motivated by love and compassion, she has made extraordinary efforts to extend his life. And, despite his age and compromised health, he has survived several near deaths. He remains alive, able to continue concluding his soul's plan for this lifetime.

Carla's love and compassion for him has taken a great emotional toll. The disruptions, challenges, and emotional tumult have left her exhausted. At times, over the last several years, the strain has left her near despondent.

Carla has a strong sense of responsibility, and she wishes to honor them. She accepts others' responsibilities as her own. She believes she is responsible for the well-being of others.

Unwavering in her determination to bravely shoulder her responsibilities, she had reached a breaking point. Her suffering prompted the unfolding of lessons that she planned to learn in this lifetime.

Change is difficult, but it is often the only thing that will free us from pain that we can no longer tolerate. Thomas' advice would show Carla a way to chart a new direction, one that would offer a better balance between care and love of others and care and love of self.

Carla is reticent to stop doing the things she doesn't want to do because of the consequences to those she loves. Her loved ones know that she must do things differently. They are not victims. If she is able to bring a balance, she will accept that her father's life and death are not in her hands. Her mother's situation is more complicated because of her emotional challenges.

You cannot spare others from the consequences of their actions forever.

Carla must recognize that not letting others be responsible for themselves does not further their soul plans. Nor does it enable their acceptance of the consequences of their actions.

If Carla is able to strike a better balance, she and her loved ones will grow more. She can delay shifting the balance, but, ultimately, this is something she will need to accomplish.

There is no way to escape the pain.

If Carla makes the changes now, she will get the relief she desires. If she delays making needed changes, her suffering will continue. As Thomas has emphasized, there is no way to avoid it.

Carla's love and compassion has exerted a heavy cost that will grow if she doesn't make the needed changes. For close to a decade, she has coped with disruptions to daily life, long distance caretaking, financial support of her husband, and the absence of any emotional support from all of the loved ones she was caring for.

Thomas' warning is stirring. If nothing changes, Carla will face the ultimate sacrifice—her life.

She runs the risk of getting sicker, so sick that she will not be able to be healed.

Carla's choice to tolerate suffering had reached a breaking point. Her strengths had become weaknesses. Her determination, sense of duty, and willingness to sacrifice herself had collided. Thomas did not gloss over the stark choices she would face in the months ahead. He had realistically prepared her for the emotional tumult that she would experience.

The months that followed were indeed difficult, as Carla established boundaries with those she loved. Although she made herself a priority, her husband, accustomed to her caretaking and support, was unable to do so. Her marriage of more than two decades ended in divorce. It would take a global pandemic to help her shift to more realistic caretaking arrangements for her parents. Forced to place practicality over emotion, she loosened the bounds her siblings had used to shift responsibility off themselves.

Carla chose to enlarge her circle of support to ride the emotional rollercoaster of change. Through therapy, spiritual counseling, and group support, she crawled her way onto the top of her priority list. While setting better boundaries is new to her, she is reaping the benefits of her efforts. She is reveling in physical and emotional health, grounded by her understanding of her spiritual journey.

She chose spiritual counseling and regression therapy, knowing intuitively that her road to peace lay in an understanding of her soul's plan for this lifetime. To achieve it, she allowed herself to be vulnerable. Doing so took great strength and bravery.

She has learned an important lesson that all must absorb. Love, care, and compassion of others must be balanced with love, care, and compassion of one's self.

As you grow emotionally and spiritually, you must learn to balance compassion for others with compassion for yourself. Self-care is an essential, yet too often overlooked, component. In fact, far too many assume that being a martyr to one's own needs is admirable. And while it may be laudable, those who prioritize the needs and wishes of others over their own do so at some peril to their well-being.

Like every other aspect of life, compassion must be balanced for the soul to grow and advance. It is foundational to developing love of self, a next step in the long journey to awaken.

The progress of our soul is like a perfect poem.
It has an infinite idea, which once realized,
makes all movements full of meaning and joy.

—RABINDRANATH TAGORE

8

Spiritual Path

After many lifetimes working on forgiveness, self-acceptance, self-worth, and self-care, you reach a point when you understand that your journey is less about your current lifetime and more about your eternal life. If you are like many others, once you have reached this point, your perspective broadens. You may live life as you always have and struggle with the same issues, but you begin to look for life's deeper meaning and purpose. You seek to reach your highest spiritual potential.

Whether you realize it or not—you are on the spiritual path.

The spiritual path is circuitous. Like other journeys, there may be roadblocks, detours, and myriad distractions that prompt you to dally. As someone once said to me, *God writes straight on crooked lines.* If that alone is not heartening, you can be comforted knowing that eternity is a very, very long time!

* * *

In the cases that follow, you will meet six people whose spiritual journey is as different as their circumstances and lives. What they do have in common is an appreciation for the fact that they are spiritual beings having a human experience.

In the first instance, we meet Rosa, whose interactions with an angelic being during her regression anchors the tumult that is robbing her inner peace and equanimity.

Rosa

Rosa is a 58-year-old research assistant at NASA. She is acutely aware that the current political environment has contributed to a general malaise. Unfortunately, this malaise has negatively impacted her emotional state. She scheduled her session to gain insight about the chaos and vitriol that is causing her and many others to feel *discombobulated.*

Rosa's experience defied expectations and provided a road map that would benefit her personally, and also her broader community.

Once in a hypnotic trance, Rosa finds herself as energy, floating within a sea of purple vastness which morphs to a brilliant gold and back again to purple. The soothing sensation leaves her feeling calm and relaxed. She is initially confused and disappointed because she is not visiting a past life as expected. She would later share that the experience she was having was more satisfying and powerful than she could ever have hoped.

She learns that her eternal name is Magda. She has had many lifetimes, most frequently incarnating as a woman, but these would be the only details about her past that she would gather.

Immersed in the sea of colors, she is joined by Archangel Michael, who is quick to offer calming words as he cradles her in an embrace of unconditional love.

Everything is okay, you need not be afraid or overly concerned.

His message is interspersed amidst a phenomenal parade of wafting colors that makes Rosa feel that she is in a distant galaxy in the center of the Universe. She knows that she is one with the colors, amidst the backdrop of a constellation of colors.

Spirals appear, a continual loop that she describes as having *no beginning and end.* The colors of purple and black are overlaid on the spirals, creating the appearance of stripes. Golden light is everywhere, intensifying with time.

She is the golden light. She carries the golden light of the Divine. The black overshadows her divinity.

Rosa understands that the fluctuation of the colors from gold to black is a visual reminder that too often she forgets she is a divine being. It is a symbol of the external tumult that has festered within her, robbing her of joy and peace.

Archangel Michael has come to remind her of her divine essence. His objective is much more important than answering the specific questions she had for the session.

Rosa continues to float in frequencies of massive colors. She witnesses the explosion of purple, yellow, gold, blue, pink, every color imaginable.

She must remember that she is a soul having a human experience and not a human having occasional spiritual experiences.

The light that emanates from her is the reminder that she is divine and that the light of her divinity radiates out.

By contrast, the chaos and tumult and suffering that you see is meant to draw your attention to the beauty of the light. There is darkness, and there is light. While things and people can appear to be dark, nothing is completely devoid of light. There is always light, even within the dark. When humans focus on the darkness, the light is overshadowed.

Rosa understands that Archangel Michael is showing her the contrast of the dark so she might better appreciate the light.

He introduces a concept that will give Rosa and many other light workers pause.

Those who are playing the dark roles have agreed to play these roles to show the contrast. They should be honored for their choice to do so.

His final words to Rosa regarding the spiritual path that she is on will resonate for some time to come. In their breadth, they are a message for all.

> *Choose the light, choose to focus on the light and not the dark. You are all beings of light, including those who have forgotten. You are all a part of the One.*

Brought up from trance, it was clear that Archangel Michael's appearance and message had an impact.

> *Wow, that was powerful!*
>
> *All I could see were the colors, the colors got bigger and bigger. Bright colors. The colors were radiating from me and swirling around me, purple, blue, pink, gold. I saw a galaxy of colors and sensed how tiny we are in this vastness.*
>
> *The light emanates from each and every one of us. This experience has reminded me of what is most important. Remaining calm and balanced amidst the chaos and vitriol is important. I can help others balance themselves through prayer and meditation.*

Rosa had been gifted with wisdom and healing. Archangel Michael reminded her that through prayer and meditation, we are beaming out our light, the light and love that is our divine essence.

The experience served to remind her to look at all the reactions she has with difficult people. In her words, *once we experience how huge we are, our small worries are dwarfed.* She left the session reminded that her current life is one in a succession of countless lifetimes. Each one a stepping-stone on the spiritual journey that began eons ago.

* * *

In the next instance, we are introduced to Yvette. Like Rosa, pain has been the driver of her spiritual growth.

YVETTE

Yvette is 50 years old and the mother of a young adult, who despite his special needs, is flourishing. This is a result of her almost single-handed efforts raising him. Throughout his childhood and youth, she voraciously sought and consumed the latest research regarding best practice therapeutic and educational techniques. During the course of caring for him, taking care of herself took the back seat.

From a low point of despair, including struggling with addiction, she reconnected to her eternal self and began actively working on aspects of her spiritual growth. It is this orientation that had her seek regression therapy.

From a prior past life regression, she knows it was during a lifetime as a priestess in Egypt that she had her closest connection to Spirit. In a recent transpersonal journey, we hear from her higher self about what weakened that connection.

> *We degrade the purity of our soul with each incarnation. If you do this often enough, your soul's purity becomes polluted. The pollution obscures your connection to God.*

Yvette is right that some souls become so disconnected that they lose sight of their connection to God. But she has forgotten that the connection is never lost.

> *When I revisited the priestess life, I felt my deep union with God. It was just so pure! From my spot on the planet, I felt connected with the Universe.*
>
> *I want and need to feel it again. I want to recapture the feeling of Home. But I can't die right now, even though I know life on the other side would be so much better. I am not done yet. I want to take care of my son.*
>
> *Now that I have chosen sobriety, I am able to have a better life.*
>
> *Overcoming the earlier struggles in my life has made me much stronger. I understand now that I can make choices about my spiritual journey. It's not all predetermined. I didn't understand that before.*

For some time, Yvette had been hoping that she could somehow pause life and the seeming endless challenges that she cycled through. Never actually contemplating suicide, she was on a long decline that might well have resulted in her death. Fear was a driving force in her pain.

Fear holds incredible power over people. We have to remember that we really have the power we need. It's not that God sends you challenges to make you stronger as we were taught as children. Fear takes form, and it holds us back. It's amazing how it changes things. I am not going to be afraid.

Yvette is joined by a cadre of healing beings. She is awash in their healing energy and love. She sighs repeatedly as she experiences the release.

Oh, oh there is so much healing.

She is reminded to call them in during her meditation whenever she needs.

I am a strong person, but I did not recognize my spiritual strength. I am going to build up my spiritual strength. I am going to release old beliefs that are no longer serving me.

Seeing a host of white angels against a beautiful deep purple background, Yvette exclaims:

I am renewing my lease on life, because I am no longer powerless! Thank you, God.

Now it's time to do the work that I have come here to do. I will work with the power of the angels.

It's not what we accomplish in one life, it's what we accomplish in the whole cycle of our lives.

In another transpersonal journey, Yvette was reminded never to forget the importance of love as the overriding emotion, something that is too often forgotten during the darkest moments and the most challenging times. The message resonates again.

When life becomes too difficult, that is when it is important to stop and connect in prayer and meditation. They are powerful tools.

What's accomplished through an earthly incarnation can't be done anywhere else. It's a choice. The individual human should be revered and loved for its heroic effort to grow spiritually through its incarnations.

Yvette embarked on a life that seemed to challenge her at every turn. At times, she was so filled with despair that she imagined her only chance of peace was for her life to end. Through hard work, she not only renewed her *lease on life,* but she reaffirmed her soul's commitment to grow spiritually.

* * *

We are next introduced to Jessica, who has embedded abandonment and patience into her life plan as a way to pursue spiritual growth.

JESSICA

Jessica is in her mid-40s, single, and very close with her mother and one sister. Her father, who abandoned the family years before, recently died. She describes the theme of abandonment as recurring in her life.

Over the last several years, she has become increasingly focused on her spiritual development. She views it as central and not tangential to her life. She scheduled a session with hopes of getting a greater understanding of the role that loss of loved ones play in her spiritual growth.

Once in trance, her higher self recounts a lifetime hundreds of years ago in which the theme of abandonment was pronounced.

As a woman in the past life, she married as a teen to the *love of her life.* Barry and she met in school and saw each other frequently in church. They lived in a small town in a tight knit community in which the church played a prominent role in people's lives. After two wonderful years together, Barry died. She was devastated by the loss, made worse by the reaction of her family and the broader community. They believed Barry's death was the *wrath of God* for her shortcomings and transgressions.

Isolated, her grief morphed to bitterness that marked her remaining life. Having lost her husband years before, she faced her own death alone.

When Barry died, I was devastated. I mourned him for a long time. I was angry at God for his death. I cursed God. I never made up with God before I died.

Looking back, she sees retrospectively that the life lessons were actually about acceptance and surrender, although at the time, she felt abandoned by her beloved, her family, community, and most devastatingly—God. It was only after she returned to soul state that she would understand the fallacy of this belief.

This was one of my first lifetimes working on surrender. I could have learned to accept that nothing is guaranteed. Had I been able to accept the loss, I would have been happier, and I probably would have met someone else.

Her focus shifts to a different life.

Jessica describes a life as a slave, in which she embedded lessons of surrender. Despite being victimized in that life, she overcompensated and was too accepting. Her oppressors convinced her that their superiority and her fate were God's intention. For the second time, she failed to strike the right balance. Worse yet, she once again allowed grossly false beliefs about God to pollute her life.

Jessica learns that one of her objectives for this lifetime is to clarify *who and what God is*. She started down that path by *stepping outside of* the religion that was such an important part of her early life. No aspect is beyond question and deliberation.

Jessica gathers an important perspective from her higher self.

You may have doubts about the overall direction for your life and want to do things differently, but, ultimately, the soul's master plan is the best plan for you to follow.

Your challenge is to be calmer about the fact that not all things are in your control. In the end, your plan will unfold even without understanding why or how. The not knowing is what makes it work. It is an important ingredient to the ultimate success of the plan. That is why surrender is important.

Discussing the seeming tug of war between control and surrender, Jessica's higher self continues.

The difficulty arises because the soul creates the plan for the upcoming life. Once you incarnate, the conscious mind doesn't have any awareness about the plan, yet you are expected to surrender. There is a tendency for the personality to want to take control, and thus you have what you call the tug of war between control and surrender.

Her higher self goes on to elaborate that she is tackling one of the most challenging aspects of surrender. Jessica is working to accept the fact that no one can control *whether they are loved or who and how they are loved.* Her father's abandonment seeded this challenge, and the recent break-up with her long-term lover advanced it.

There is no guarantee that your romantic partner could be everything to you.

Your search for love is too narrow. You confuse it with your desire for a romantic partner. Love takes many forms. There are other ways that people express their love that you dismiss: friends, mentors, all the other people who love you and meet your needs. Once you get a more balanced perspective, you will be on the right track.

Jessica's higher self affirms that when the conscious mind is able to accept the idea of a divine plan, the personality is able to relax and stop struggling.

Struggling with patience is a clue that more work on surrender needs to be done. You will find as you are able to surrender to the divine plan, you will no longer be so impatient. You will have stepped outside of earthly time.

Jessica's higher self reminds her of the benefits of living each day with gratitude.

Constantly find things to be thankful for. Be actively grateful in your statements, your actions, in your prayers and meditation. When you are grateful for the life you have, you stop focusing on the things and life that you don't have.

In words that would resonate long into the future, Jessica's higher self gifted her with a message of encouragement.

> *You agreed to this plan because you knew you could do it. It will facilitate your spiritual growth.*

Upon return to full consciousness, Jessica shared how relevant the session was and how much more relaxed and at ease she felt.

> *There was a certain point where you can feel the size of your body, and yet you are beyond the limits of your body, as if it didn't exist. You are the observer who is watching the melding of two different worlds, the outer world and the inner world.*
>
> *Wow!*
>
> *It was so clear. You have all of this knowledge and insight showering down on you, but you can't even verbalize it. I don't know how to capture it using human words.*
>
> *In the trance, I was reminded of some of the relatively new things I have been learning about the spiritual journey. I got what I needed… my path forward.*

* * *

Yvette and Jessica are not alone in having acquired false beliefs about God and their eternal nature. In the next two instances, we meet Kayla and Arjun. Both were traumatized by the misgivings and misinformation they acquired lifetimes ago about the Source of all light and love.

Kayla

Kayla is a 52-year-old editor who transitioned to part-time work so that she might pursue her interest in spirituality and metaphysics. She has been married to her college sweetheart for more than two decades and is mother to two young adults.

Kayla has experienced a sense of detachment and emotional abandonment that appears incompatible with her history of relationships with family members and friends. By her own description, her heart is shut down. She describes herself as loveable but invisible, reflecting a perceived imbalance in her relations with others.

I give myself to everyone, without leaving enough for myself. I am beginning to focus on myself.

When we first met, Kayla had started meditating a year before and was hoping to connect with others who were also pursuing spiritual interests. Her meditation practice had spawned a desire to grow spiritually and to connect more directly with her spirit guides. At an intellectual level, she knows that she is divine. She admitted that she longs to feel it on an emotional level. She sensed that something is blocking the experience.

Some months later, Kayla scheduled her first past life regression. While the experience piqued her metaphysical interests, it did not offer any clarity or direction. In the ensuing months, the sense of abandonment deepened, as did her conviction that her heart was frozen. Her second regression a year and a half later would provide the clarity and direction she desired.

Once in trance, Kayla finds herself in a garden setting where she connects with her higher self. Her eternal name is Ellie, who is pleased to share.

We have a fear of not doing our best, a fear of letting others down. We also fear not being accepted into the Divine light. This possibility makes us sad.

I don't know how this started, but it feels like we've been shut out. We were told we were not good enough. If we do things that are wrong, that's another reason to not be accepted. It's easier to not do anything. But we don't like that.

Kayla is dependable because that's the right thing to do. She helps people because she wants to do it and not because it is what other people want or expect from her.

The worst thing we've ever been through is the feeling of just never being good enough. It feels like it has been through all lifetimes.

In the past, demands were ever-present and overwhelming. It's never enough. You can't do your best, so you just give in. You don't stick-up for yourself. You don't know who to turn to for help. Who do you trust?

Ellie begins discussing a lifetime thousands of years ago when she dwelled in a cave with an abusive partner. He was a brute, much stronger than her. Her only joy was her animals.

During that life, my partner beat me. He said I wasn't good enough. I felt imprisoned. Nobody wants to be beaten, it doesn't feel good. He was so angry. As life became harder and harder, he took his anger out on me. It was easier for him to take the anger out on me than to find a solution.

Survival was not ensured. He had trouble providing for us. He would share me sexually with other men, trading me for essentials that we needed. It was easier for him to give me away than struggle to provide.

We lived alone, and I was isolated. There was no community. I couldn't leave. It wasn't safe. It was too scary a world to be out alone. It was the price I had to pay for being protected.

I wished I had a better life, but I felt trapped. I couldn't leave. I accepted the idea that this was what I had to do. I didn't live a long life.

Ellie abruptly shifts focus. She is now discussing a life she had in medieval England. Despite how different the outer experience of life was, the connection between the prehistoric and medieval lives is apparent.

I am in another time and life. I am a wealthy woman. We live a safe and comfortable life. Our royal status ensures that my needs are provided for.

I am overwhelmed because it seems that everyone wants something from me. People beg at my feet asking for things. I can't find even one person that just wants me. I'm not enough!

I wasn't able to be with the man I loved because of my father. He gave me to another man to advance his position and political status. It wasn't a harsh life, but it was one in which I didn't have any say over myself. I felt like a prisoner in my husband's home. I loved my children. I accepted my situation so that my children would not suffer.

I never saw my beloved again. My heart was broken. I was angry at God and blamed God for the fact that I couldn't choose how to live my life.

Choice is a big part of Kayla's current life.

When I incarnated as a man, I had some choice over my life. In my many lives as a woman, until now, I have had none. There has been a significant power imbalance between men and women.

She moves to the end of her life, and in soul state, Ellie shares.

I wish I had bettered myself. I regret not having taken any risks nor standing up for myself. I originally felt like I had power, and then it was gone, taken away from me by my father and the circumstances of the times. I didn't have much power, and I feared losing the little I had. On top of that, everyone was just wanting me to give. No one was giving.

I'm tired of giving to everybody else and not taking care of me.

The higher self realizes that her disgust for the incessant grasping by others was symbolic of what she had been denied—personal power. The connection between the most recent life and the life millennia before has been clarified. She experienced the loss of power as a loss of self. With access to her memories of that life, she adds.

I know that if I had escaped, I would have faced danger and an uncertain future. But I feel as if I could have found a way out. Maybe I didn't work hard enough, didn't do enough. I didn't believe in myself.

There have been other lives in which I didn't get what I needed. Giving people what they wanted, making them happy, became my norm, even when it was to my own detriment and sacrifice. I became very accommodating. It's been a pattern for a long time.

I can't remember when I began to believe that I wasn't enough. I think it began during the lifetime millennia ago.

I may have had wealth, comfort, and status in the royal life, but I never felt like I was enough. Its deeper than the outer trappings of how I lived. It's about how I felt about myself.

What I wanted or what I expressed didn't matter.

I must not be important, because I'm not heard. What I think, say, or do isn't valued. And now it just seems like this is the way it was always meant to be. I have not been heard in many lives.

My father's decision broke my heart. What I said didn't matter. What I wanted didn't matter. What was important to me didn't matter. And I felt too powerless to run away.

When I can't find a way, I just conform to the choices others make for me. Instead of fighting against it or even running away, if that's appropriate, I acquiesce.

Ellie admits that she may be angry at herself for the choices she has made and acknowledges that this has combined with her anger at women's position within society.

My opinion didn't matter. I was just a body that can be given to someone else. That's how both my dad and my partner made me feel.

Although the connection between the two lives that Ellie has revisited is clear, what is not clear is the origin of the beliefs she holds, not being good enough nor having value. Even her mistreatment in prehistoric times does not fully explain beliefs that have remained solidified for thousands of years.

Hoping to clear some of the anger and frustration that may be blocking full understanding, Ellie agrees to let me call-in the soul of her father in the medieval lifetime. Through tears, she tells him:

My voice matters. Going against my wishes is going against who I am. It violates me, my heart, and my love. Losing the man I loved wasn't even the worst part. It was the fact that you took my value away from me.

I matter. My opinion matters. I am important enough to be heard.

I can make my own decisions. You can support me in those decisions and not threaten me. I never saw my beloved again. My heart was broken. I blamed you and God for the fact that I couldn't choose how to live my life.

Ellie's father is remorseful.

I'm sorry, it was the way it was. It wasn't about you. It was about what we had to do to get what was needed at the time.

Despite accepting her father's apology, Ellie remains distressed.

I think Kayla does a really good job forgiving all the trespasses against her, maybe too easily. Even though I feel like I had forgiven him, I still carry all this angst and anxiety. I carry the burden of not feeling valued and not good enough to be listened to. Kayla is carrying this lack of value. She second-guesses herself.

Searching for insight about these beliefs, I ask Ellie to explain why she blamed God.

I thought if I did all the things I was supposed to do, that God wanted me to do, I would have God's love and protection. I felt like God abandoned me in hundreds of lifetimes. I believed that if you worked hard enough, prayed hard enough, and did the right thing, then you would not get punished. When you do things that are bad, God punishes you. I felt like I was punished.

I'm not good enough, so I have no voice. I'm guilty for not doing enough and being good enough. When you're mean or hurt other people or do things against other people, you are prompting God's rejection. We were all taught not to do that stuff. I haven't measured up. I believe I am being punished for not living up to God's standards.

Finally, we had uncovered the power behind the negative thoughts Kayla holds about her life and herself.

The higher self believes that all of the things that have happened to her across many lifetimes are a result of God's wrath for not being good enough. She believes that God has a standard for behavior that she has failed to measure-up to. And that is the origin of her guilt. Not feeling lovable is the label for not measuring up to God's expectations.

Her early lives of mistreatment left her feeling fearful, unsafe, and not in control. She concluded that God must have been displeased with her because no one came to her rescue. This instilled lots of fear, anger, and guilt. It left her feeling abandoned and with a strong sense of unworthiness. Her desire to get back in God's good graces led her in an incessant cycle of doing everything to please and satisfy others.

Drowning in disappointment, she turned her anger inward. She internalized the images of a wrathful, unforgiving God who in his disgust issues a life-sentence, in fact—many life-sentences.

The higher self realized that to repair her disconnection with God, she would need a corrective action plan. So, she embedded strengthening the connection to God in the soul plan she crafted for Kayla's lifetime.

People struggle for decades trying to reconcile what they have been taught about God. Formulating new ideas in order to write a new script about the Divine is not as simple as writing a term paper on the subject. In unearthing the long-held false beliefs that her higher self held across millennia, Kayla gained understanding, emotional relief, and clarity about her spiritual journey. Now, she is working on reinforcing the belief that God loves and accepts her.

> *I chose to come into a family that chose to break away from traditional religious dogma. I am free to release limiting beliefs and to come to know God directly. My relationship with God will be based on who and what I am. Now, I see that we are all accepted. We don't have to do certain things or act in certain ways.*
>
> *The life themes make so much sense. Since I began focusing on spiritual matters, I have been working to form a new opinion about God. I now see that I am free to choose what to believe about God, and through meditation, directly connect.*

Over millennia, there have been myriad efforts to create and peddle a wrathful God. Few promoted the image of a loving and unconditionally accepting God. Rarely have people been reminded of their own divine essence. Today we are indeed fortunate that there is guidance and encouragement to directly connect to God.

* * *

In this next case, we meet Arjun, who, like Kayla, has suffered because of falsely framed beliefs about God. In his case, those beliefs were a result of fallacy passed on by a well-intentioned but misinformed spiritual teacher.

Arjun

Arjun is a 50-year-old chemical engineer. He is devoutly religious, and Hinduism assumes a prominent place in his life. He has been married for 24 years and has three beautiful teenage daughters. He is devoted to his beloved wife and daughters, which is particularly relevant given the reason for his interest in regression therapy.

Arjun shared that he had been yelling at his wife and daughters for several months prior to arranging a past life regression session. He described his behavior as out of character, inexplicable, as well as inappropriate. Worried that it was negatively impacting their previously harmonious home life, he was anxious to uncover the reasons for his verbal explosions.

Once in trance, Arjun finds himself floating in an undefined space. He died at 82 after a long and happy life as a farmer in India in the ninth century. He had a wife, two sons and daughters-in-law, and five grandchildren.

He knows that he has been dead for a long time and offers the following explanation about his choice to not move into the light.

> *The stillness stopped me. I was attracted to the beauty of the stillness. This is what I expected it would be like when my life ended. I stayed in the stillness for more than 400 years. I had been taught that the stillness was perfection.*

Despite luxuriating in the stillness, eventually, Arjun's soul became *bored,* which led him to question whether in fact *stillness* was the *perfection* his religion had taught. He understood that within the stillness he would also *experience love,* but this was clearly not the case. The absence of anything other than stillness eventually led to frustration. His efforts to suppress his frustration turned into anger, which also had to be repressed.

Over the course of his time in the stillness, other souls came by who were similarly frustrated at their circumstances. Their commiserations relieved some of the frustration, but all these years later, Arjun's soul still seethed with anger.

Eventually, he began to wonder whether his spiritual teachers had been wrong. Although the others who passed by were similarly confused, Arjun's soul blamed himself for misunderstanding and not the teachers for failed teachings.

> *I was taught never to question, to have faith. Those who question are considered nonbelievers. Nonbelievers go to hell. Those doomed to hell, boil in oil.*
>
> *It was easier to blame myself for misunderstanding.*

Questioning religious tenets and leaders was a dangerous proposition!

According to Arjun's higher self, sometime in the 12th century, Lord Shiva came to rescue him.

> *Shiva said, it's time to go.*
>
> *Later, I was reborn in Tuyet, the town that I lived in as a farmer. I was able to pick my family. My criteria for selecting them was they should want to seek salvation.*
>
> *Before the new life, I was also allowed to study with Reameanea, a spiritual guide, to clarify the misunderstandings. I was taught to seek salvation through practice and experience, including through prayer and meditation. He taught me that within salvation, I would find stillness and love, including love of others, but not love of self.*
>
> *I was helped to let go of the frustration but not the anger. My anger was immense. I had been cheated out of 400 years!*

While much had been clarified, Arjun's soul would begin his new incarnation in Tuyet with a mixed bag of beliefs. On the positive side, he understood that his God—Brahman—is love, and that love is one and the same as salvation. Sadly, he was left believing that self-love is bad and that he is not worthy enough to be loved.

Both of these beliefs created worry that salvation is beyond his reach and are reflected in the previous inexplicable outbursts in his current life.

With hope of clearing up century old beliefs, I invited those who Arjun worships to connect. Arjun is joined by the Hindu God Shiva and Saint Vivekananda. They wrap him in a loving embrace and release the anger that has festered unhealed for centuries.

They remind him to *follow the path of meditation and prayer.*

Before leaving, Brahman tells Arjun.

> *You too are divine. You should honor and love yourself as you love and honor others. In doing so, you are a role model for others and an ambassador for me.*

Awash in the power of this divine love, Arjun notes that peace has replaced the space previously filled with his anger and frustration. In closing, he shares his new prayer.

> *I love and honor myself, and in doing so, I radiate the Divine.*

People are surprised to learn in regression that they may have delayed crossing over in a previous life. There are many reasons. The insight gleaned from such a discovery can be invaluable.

Arjun's failure to cross into the light, while exceptional, is not unique. There are many circumstances that lead souls to dally or to consciously choose not to move into the interlife. What is important about this and other instances, is that discovering what led to that decision may be relevant in your current life. For Arjun it was a composite of misinformation about eternal life, remnants of which he still held at the time of his session.

Arjun's soul brought the energy and beliefs from his traumatic experience into this life for resolution. Interestingly, a new priest espousing a different spiritual philosophy at his temple was the trigger for Arjun's eruptions with his family.

Many things can inhibit our connection to God. The most common is the belief that God has caused or failed to prevent a devastating tragedy. In Arjun's case, it was a misinformed belief that interfered. But whatever the disruption, we are never truly separated from God.

The soul is a brilliant choreographer of circumstances that lead to desired healing and learning. Humans tend to be motivated to change through upheaval and contrast, which the soul happily orchestrates to enhance growth. When subtle clues are ignored, the soul's clamor for change becomes louder, until the need for change can no longer be ignored.

In a case such as this with so many variables, it might be too easy to miss what is the most valuable nugget for all—Braham's reminder to Arjun that he is divine, and as such is worthy of self-love.

This is a universal truth. You have been made in the image and likeness of God, birthed as an individuated expression and experience of the Creator. As such, you, like Arjun, are divine. And just like Arjun, you are worthy of self-love.

* * *

We next meet Linh, who has reached the point on her spiritual path in which developing love of self takes center stage.

LINH

Linh is a 40-years-old financial manager who is also an adept energy healer. Her family emigrated to the United States when she was a toddler and, like many families in similar circumstances, experienced isolation. Her older brother was a major positive force in her development while her parents worked tirelessly to establish their family in their new home country.

Linh had been briefly married. A second, significant relationship ended amicably after a move left Linh and her lover thousands of miles apart. A year later, she discovered that she could communicate telepathically with him while meditating.

Several months before scheduling her first session, she had the first of numerous mystical experiences conversing with Kuan Yin, the Chinese Goddess of compassion. For decades, Kuan Yin has been a prominent spiritual figure for her family.

Linh approached her life between lives sessions seeking to understand her purpose in life, the soul agreements she made, and her capacity to heal others energetically.

In her first regression, she experiences herself as an energy being and finds herself amidst a cadre of light beings. Her guide Atera joins in.

She is being schooled in different healing techniques using her hands. This capacity will provide joy as she shares it with others.

Her empathic abilities serve her well. She can learn to heal herself. She just needs to listen to the messages. When she learns to heal herself, she will be better able to heal others. She may end up working as a healer, engaging and helping more and more people in this way.

Later, Atera reminds her that she is in the process of rising from darkness that resulted from prior lives as a warrior. He emphasizes the importance of her learning to love herself again.

This thread reappears in her life between lives session a month later.

Linh's plan for this lifetime is to experience and learn through love. She has made soul agreements with others to help her do this. Her relationship with her brother was planned to teach her familial love. Her marriage expanded upon that teaching. It also provided her with chances to develop boundaries, recognize her strengths, and develop self-love. Other relationships with family members, colleagues, and friends expanded the opportunities for refining her understanding of love.

Atera highlights some of the nuanced aspects of love.

Everything that is touched by love becomes calm and peaceful. There is joy when love is exchanged. But there are also instances when one person loves another and that love is not reciprocated. Even then, the person who loves the other can experience joy.

Atera continues, hoping that Linh will grasp the dual experience of love, the joy of loving another, and the joy of being loved by that same person.

In this instance, if you can detach from any expectation that your love of another will be reciprocated, you retain the joy you experience loving them. While you can't pursue a relationship at that point, you can still cherish your love for the person. Minimizing it is a disservice to yourself. The joy of loving is marred by attachment and grasping. If you can remove all of this, you are left just with the joy. This helps when your partner dies or leaves. Understanding that you are eternal also mitigates the loss of the physical presence of a love.

Contemporary cultures romanticize love, but it is much more than that. Romantic love can be smothering. Physical attraction combined with love can be very powerful and overwhelming for some. It creates a deep bond. But you have to guard against being blinded by the attraction.

Atera explains how understanding the nature of love is important for Linh to learn to love herself.

The negative relationships that Linh has had were to teach her about love. Initially, the complexities clouded her understanding of love. Ultimately, they helped her remember that she is love. She needed to learn to care for herself. Like each of you, she is worthy and deserving of that care.

Love is important for connection, to achieve oneness. Love is expansive and is connected to all things.

To fully experience her divinity, Linh must learn to love herself.

As many have said, the experience of awakening to your divine essence, to the love within, is an experience that is beyond words. Words fail to express the ecstasy of connection. The road home starts with the desire to remember that you are divine.

Self-love sets the stage.

* * *

EDWARD

A similar message about our divine essence was echoed by Kelly's spirit guide Edward who we met in Chapter Two.

It is hard for humans to remember their innate worth. Humans, as an act of hubris, have attempted through time to control and put down other humans by exploiting divinity. Some, with an exaggerated sense of their self-worth and power, manipulated others through religion, chipping away at their sense of self-worth. This is why so many have forgotten their divine essence.

Humanity needs to remember that we are all from the same spark. We are all one. This thought had been lost for ages but is now reemerging slowly through the infusion of enlightened individuals.

This reawakening can be helped by those who spread this reminder through small groups and connecting one on one. Connecting in these ways enables participants to experience their own divinity directly. Embracing meditation will help to advance spiritually.

The need for this awakening has led us to send additional help. There are enlightened individuals who are spreading the word. It is all around you. It can be seen in everyday life and interactions, in books, in movies that carry this important message.

Edward's words are a powerful reminder.

Perhaps you too are awakening to your eternal nature and destiny. Understanding that you are first and foremost a spiritual being having a human lifetime is an essential step in your spiritual growth. Equally important is understanding that you are on the path to embodying unconditional love and acceptance.

But these ideas alone are not sufficient. To reach full realization, you must overcome the emotional challenges that have robbed you of peace and joy, including loss, forgiveness, self-acceptance, doubt, self-worth and self-care. Doing so requires that you rout out the false beliefs that previously caused so much pain and prompted actions that didn't serve your highest purpose. The physical, emotional, and spiritual benefits of accomplishing this are significant and worth the effort.

If you don't love yourself, you cannot love others.
You will not be able to love others.
If you have no compassion for yourself,
then you are not able to develop compassion for others.

—DALAI LAMA

9

DEEPENING YOUR CAPACITY TO LOVE

Deepening your capacity to love is central to emotional and spiritual growth. It necessitates self-acceptance, which is based on your ability to overcome doubt and to forgive yourself for past failings or transgressions. It includes trusting yourself. It involves honoring yourself for who you have become and for all that you have been through, challenges overcome, and victories achieved, whether small or large. It requires dispelling the illusion that you ever needed to earn your value and instead come to realize that you had intrinsic worth all along. It then entails applying these lessons and prioritizing and caring for yourself, learning to say no, and setting boundaries.

Your deepened capacity to love eventually blossoms into self-love. It is neither easily achieved nor permanent and must itself be cultivated and reinforced. But once you have reached this point, you begin to awaken to your divine essence.

* * *

In the cases that follow, you will see the importance of self-love and the role it plays in the process of deepening your capacity for love.

But first, we hear from Destiny's spirit guide who tantalizes with the bliss that awaits as you awaken to your divine essence.

Destiny

Demetri, a spirit guide working with a woman named Destiny, offered the following to further an understanding about awakening one's divine essence.

Yes, you are correct that God is absolute love.

It is God's intention that you manifest love through your relationships. God works through people, not things, and thus interactions are essential. It is intended that through these associations you will connect as one.

As humans, you are sent into life to have interactions with others, to learn to love yourselves so that you can remember your divine essence. That's why you are created.

Human interactions and relationships provide an excellent way to develop your capacity for love. They offer an opportunity to learn about love and how to function within the continuum of love. Doing so brings you closer to God.

You need to remove emotional blocks, as well as stop being afraid. You need to learn to be okay with yourself. Self-acceptance is important. Stop being dismissive of yourself. Learn to value and trust yourself.

Demetri's parting words amplify his earlier more practical advice.

Each person holds the energy of a supernova. Feel that connection. So much change can happen if you connect to it.

* * *

In this next case, we are introduced to Gabriella. Like Linh, who you met in the previous chapter, her soul plan has been designed to deepen her capacity for love by learning self-love.

GABRIELLA

Gabriella is a 42-year-old human resource manager who is planning to launch her own professional development firm. She is single, after an eight-year relationship with Ian ended. It had been her hope that they would marry. This most recent loss cascaded on her father's abandonment decades ago, leaving her distraught and struggling to comprehend the spiritual lessons she had planned for this lifetime.

In the first of a series of sessions, Gabriella visits a past life on the American plains in the early 19th century. Early in life she established herself as strong, courageous, and fiercely independent. Her life was filled with many richly rewarding experiences before marrying in her mid-forties. Her husband became gravely ill. This caused panic and fear that he would die before her. She is aware her worries seem incongruous with the independent spirit that has been the hallmark of her life.

In soul state, she is greeted by her soul friends who are laughing, saying *see, we told you so.* The inference does not escape her. She remembers that she is still trying to heal from an even earlier life in which she died very young. It was a happy life in which she had planned to accomplish great things, but tragically, it was cut short. She notes.

> *I am being held back. Death is cheating me. Either I die before my time, or someone I love dies before I am ready to lose them. It's just not fair! There is this bigger plan, but I don't know what it is. I just wish I knew. I just want to make sense of the bigger plan. My guide tells me I must be patient, but I'm impatient.*

Gabriella's higher self admits that she sometimes wonders *what is the point of living* and *what is the point of loving* if it leads to loss. She sees how in her current life these beliefs may be playing out.

> *I'm always scared that if I love someone too much, they will die.*

At the same time, Gabriella's higher self acknowledges that she needs to be more patient and accept that she can't control everything. Strength and courage will enable obstacles to be overcome.

Gabriella returned several weeks later for her life between lives session. She moves easily into a deep trance. In the womb before birth, her higher self shares that her upcoming life will be filled with challenges. But it will also be a life in which she will find happiness.

> *I know that I will set an example for others and help people understand what love really is.*

Other details unfold as the session progresses.

Before moving into the interlife, she briefly visits a past life on a Caribbean Island. She is a man named John living with his wife. They are slaves on a sugar plantation. Their two small children were taken and sold as slaves and sent away.

> *We will be killed if we rise up.*

John moves ahead to his last day. He is 50 years old and lays dying of an infection in the presence of his loving wife. Released from his agony, he floats out of his body. Looking back on his life, he shares:

> *I feel satisfied with my life. Although I wasn't free, I chose to be kind to others and did not wallow in anger. I learned how to be happy despite my external circumstances.*

Reaching the interlife, Gabriella meets her spirit guide Scion. She learns that she has had 70 lifetimes, mostly on earth. She sees the five souls who are a part of her study group. They are very close and have been working together for some time.

We hear from her higher self.

> *We are working on understanding love and acceptance. We formed as a group to study the theme of love. We have been studying it for a long time. We all have different views. My view is different from the conventional understanding of what love is.*

I am exploring how labels change our expectations of love. Outside of those labels, we must allow love to take its own shape and form. It includes acceptance. For example, if I call someone my spouse, it comes with certain expectations and obligations that should not be a part of what love is. Because love is freedom, and it is also truly accepting people for who they are and not trying to change them.

Love cannot be defined by one thing, one person, or one view. It has many sides, both good and bad.

In my prior life as the slave John, I was looking for perspective on how to feel empathy toward someone who did not know what he was doing. It took me a while to work through my feelings of anger and my beliefs that it was unfair. Eventually, I realized that he just didn't know any better.

I had to learn acceptance and forgiveness toward those who took and enslaved my children. I overcame my bitterness because I knew that otherwise it would lead to continued suffering.

After this lengthy discussion with Gabriella's higher self, Scion shares his view on her soul's plan relative to love and relationships. His *tough love* approach to being a guide becomes apparent as he matter-of-factly rattles off a long list of challenges facing Gabriella.

She wants to learn not to place expectations on others and to let others be free to take their own journeys. She needs to be less impatient. She needs to let go of the desire to control outcomes. She has trouble understanding and making sense of the bigger plan and would like to control things more.

She hopes and wants things to happen on a certain schedule. But the more she gets impatient, the longer it will take her to advance her patience. It's about learning to let go and to be patient.

This incarnation is an opportunity to work on love. The experience of losing love is just another way that you learn about love.

Through Scion's comments, Gabriella has come to understand that dying of a broken heart in a past life is just one example of a way that we learn to deepen our capacity to love. So too is a life in which love is lost through death or abandonment. There are many other examples, and all are opportunities to learn about love in relationship with another. As we do so, our capacity for love deepens.

With prodding, Scion adds.

In her relationship with Ian, she worked very hard on these lessons and has made a lot of progress. She will have a lifelong partner when the time is right.

Gabriella secured an understanding about her life plan and how it fits within her soul's eternal interest and journey. She uncovered specific information about the spiritual lessons she had planned for this lifetime and the cohorts who are helping her acquire this wisdom.

Although the hope of finding a life partner was reinforced, she was frustrated that the detail on this was limited. She knows that patience is not yet a strong suit.

Although she experienced Scion as far from warm and comforting, she found his insights valuable. With his help, her current struggles and disappointments were placed into context.

In the future, understanding what her soul hoped she would accomplish in this lifetime will serve her well. She knows to achieve this she will need to step back and allow her higher self to direct her decisions and actions.

Like many, Gabriella's experience with love has been in relationship to the others who she has loved. Although she and her soul group are working to understand love and acceptance of others, they have yet to learn self-love. As she deepens her capacity to love, loving herself will take center stage.

* * *

Ishtok, who is Gwen's spirit guide, both of whom we met in Chapter Five, offered his thoughts on this very issue.

There is a difference between the love you experience as a human and the love you experience at Home. For the majority, human love manifests as familial, romantic, or friendship. In terms of romantic love, you have the added influence of the sexual energy. The mix can intensify both the yearning and grasping.

There are some who can bring the higher, unconditional love from Home into human life. There is a sweetness to it when this happens.

In the world of contrast on Earth, this is a much more challenging thing to experience. Conditional love is relevant in the earthly world and necessary to help you make decisions, to know right and wrong. Unconditional love is relevant in the spirit realm. Both are precious.

The remembrance of unconditional love from the spirit realm leads humans to yearn for it and in turn to try and find it in their relationships. They look for it, but it is very rare to find it. Even though the sweetness of unconditional love cannot be experienced fully on earth, the recall of its joy and wonder fuel incessant searches.

During incarnation, we are educated by our group. We are told what is good and what is bad. We also come in with memories that are imprinted in the history of the lineage of our DNA. You come into human life to work on certain things. Confidence, for example, is a sign of self-love. Fears are a reflection of the lack of self-love. You combine these things together, and you can understand the challenges to being able to love yourself in this realm.

It's a decision that must be made by the person to accept whatever the circumstances that lead them to a lack of love. If, for instance, they made some mistake but refused to accept that they did the best they could, that is an example of not being able to love oneself.

In the spirit world, there is just no problem with that. We are showered with love. Even when we come back broken, we are showered in love from the Divine. Self-love is not a challenge in the interlife.

There are millions who have yet to awaken to their divine essence. Remembering is not automatic. It takes motivation and concerted effort across many lifetimes. Many things get in the way. Some are struggling to survive. Others are working to overcome challenges or trauma. While still others are distracted by the joys of the human adventure on earth.

Regardless of your individual pace, you can be comforted knowing that the journey you set out on eons ago is destined for success. Whether you dally in the joy of earthly distractions or get confused and lost because of mishaps and setbacks, know that your final destination is one and the same. As your capacity for love deepens, you will begin to realize and awaken to your divinity and the peace and happiness that is its essence.

* * *

Even those who are well along their spiritual path must continually work to balance love and compassion for others with love and compassion for self. The next case is instructive in this regard.

FRANCESCA

Francesca is a 60-years-old corporate consultant. She is very close to her one daughter and sister and is very involved with members of her large extended family. This has been the source of both joy and frustration, given the natural tendency of adults to welcome but not follow others' advice. Her marriage ended years before. Her desire for a long-term relationship has not manifested and has been the source of disappointment.

She was raised in a structured religion that she rejected, given its rigidity, but she is highly spiritually oriented and motivated.

Six years ago, she left her career in health care, guided by her sense that she was meant to help others progress on their spiritual journeys. Although she freely counsels others about spiritual matters, her interest in making this a career focal point has yet to manifest.

She has had several regressions, including transpersonal journeys, past life, and life between lives sessions over the course of several years, coupled with spiritual counseling. Most sessions focused on securing spiritual guidance relative to life decisions and overcoming general feelings of malaise.

At times, a sense that she has not fully realized her soul's plan for this lifetime has left her anguished. It is also clear she has carried forward the guilt that in prior lives she failed to live up to a set of standards that few humans could meet.

Of her numerous regressions, her life between lives session offered the greatest insight about the interrelationship of these topics. The wisdom she gleaned from this session built on the information from several past lives in which she was a spiritual teacher and leader.

Given her experience, Francesca easily moves into trance. She reports from her vantage point within her mother's womb that her higher self chose to wait until immediately before birth to join with the fetus. She has selected a family to be born into that will force her to become more independent. In prior lives, she has been suffocated by tradition and rules.

Even in the womb, she knows that as her life unfolds, there will be many challenges to realizing her soul's plan.

> *I am supposed to bring the light to help others escape pain and fear. I am supposed to teach others how to let go. I am supposed to demonstrate love, to show love, to be love. We need to fight to bring the light. The light brings freedom.*

Her perspective expands to include the experience of her life to date.

> *I thought it would be easier, but it wasn't. They bound me. They held on tight. They said I was wrong. They threatened me. They said I could not be myself and do what I wanted. But I knew that independence is important.*

Francesca experiences a brief recall of a past life and then arrives in the interlife. She is welcomed by her spirit guide Sara and several high beings.

She identifies her spiritual purpose, a path of service.

> *I have a very strong knowing that I am to help others. To teach others to be strong, especially those who have had horrible experiences in life. I am very strong. I want to do for others. I want to work with those who have not done well in prior lives.*

Francesca's desire to help others is not without a cost to her. She has modeled strength through adversity so that others might learn to do so. The result has been personal suffering.

> *When I suffer in this lifetime, it is to show others that we are not alone, and we are not to give up.*

We learn from Sara that in this lifetime, Francesca is working to balance her compassion for others and compassion for herself.

> *She is learning to balance, to let go, and release all of her suffering. Through her own growth, she will continue to be a role model for others on their spiritual journey.*
>
> *Francesca can help those who are ready to open their minds and hearts to learn about their own spiritual paths.*
>
> *She is angry, feeling that she has been held back from accomplishing her mission. This has caused her much pain and disappointment. She is disappointed with those she has helped, believing that many are not progressing spiritually. She needs to suspend judgement and to learn to let go of her expectations of others. She needs to accept.*

Sara notes that Francesca had lost sight of the fact that others are free to choose. In lifetime after lifetime, her efforts failed to yield similar results. Wrongly, she had internalized the failure of others to advance spiritually. The work that she began several years before to fortify herself is producing results. Hers is not a solitary mission. It is one shared by a legion of lightworkers and *reinforcements are on the way!*

> *Francesca is driven by spiritual love. Her search for a loving partner in this lifetime has been frustrating. She has always focused on spiritual love and connections. At times, her plan was to include grand romantic loves, but her focus is always her spiritual work. Francesca's deep desire to be in communion with Source has triumphed over her search for romantic love.*
>
> *But soon she will find someone. It is time for her to have a partner, someone who will care for and support her. She will no longer need to worry or struggle. They will share friendship, companionship, and love. She will be free to spread her light and to bring others to the light.*
>
> *Humans forget their spiritual nature and get confused trying to replicate their connection to Source in relationships with other humans. When they follow society and tradition, they are told that they will find a great love and marry. That is an experience of the human personality, but it falls short of the experience of divine love. They are seeking to re-experience fully the love of the Divine. This desire motivates the search to find human love. It is an attempt to create what is experienced when they return Home.*

Francesca chose to share the depth of the Divine's love with others through her many lives of service. She suffered greatly due to her dedication to others. The belated decision to prioritize her own needs over the last several years is finally achieving balance.

Perhaps you too have shared this view of what following a spiritual path means. Maybe you have embodied the tenets of a religion that holds that your suffering serves others. If so, like Francesca, you may view your own needs and desires as unimportant.

What's important to remember here is that the path to self-love requires balance. It entails having love and compassion for yourself, as well as for your loved ones and the greater humanity. Perhaps an easy question to lead you to your answer is the one I pose to my clients.

Would you treat God the way you treat yourself?

The honest answer to this question may help accelerate your own spiritual journey and final return Home.

* * *

In this next section, we hear from another spirit guide regarding the importance of developing self-love.

Anthony

In his counsel to Anthony, another client I have worked with, his spirit guide lovingly refers to souls as particles.

Self-love is an appreciation of the particle of God that you oversee. You are its guardian. Unless you start appreciating that you are part of God, you cannot appreciate the other particles. It must be a full appreciation of who you are, without the other extreme of selfishness. It is a very subtle difference, appreciating who you are without thinking of yourself as separate from all else.

Self-love includes appreciating yourself as part of everything, and as everything, not seeing yourself as separate. You should love yourself as you love the Universe. You will naturally love yourself if you can stop making a distinction between yourself and the Universe.

Mastering self-love can be tricky because there is a risk of becoming selfish. As you develop love for yourself, you should concurrently pursue love for other individuals and humanity along with love for the Universe and the oneness. These are natural processes that should be done in parallel.

There is no separation, no border between loving yourself and loving others. Once you understand that you are one with others, then love for yourself flows naturally. Loving yourself and loving others is all the same. Conversely, if you hate yourself and you constantly criticize or punish yourself, you cannot truly love others. Acceptance is important.

Like many others, Anthony has just forgotten that he is one with the Universe. And when he separates himself from the Universe, he has lost his connection to the love. Separation is undermining his self-love. He must remember the interconnection.

In a sense, it is concentrating on the oneness through his spiritual practice that will keep him loving himself.

This brief exchange has underscored the need to find balance, including between your love of self and love of others. It is also a reminder to not lose sight that loving relationships are a vehicle for getting the balance right.

If you were asked to name all the people and things that you love, how long might it take you to name yourself? Imagine how different your life might be if you focused on what you love about yourself. Or, if you understood that how you love yourself is how you teach others to love you.

* * *

In the following case, we are introduced to Maryam. Her impatience to awaken fully into her divine essence resulted in a soul plan that is as challenging as it is unusual. Ignoring the counsel of the higher beings, her personality is now left to cope with the pain and longing that are an outgrowth of her life plan.

Maryam

Maryam is a 51-year-old, married, cardiac surgeon. Several years ago, during surgical rounds at the hospital, she felt an immediate strong connection with one of the residents. His name is Daniel.

> *It was as if we were already dear, close friends. I had felt a similar sense of connection before with one of my closest friends, but the experience with Daniel was more intense. I felt a deep romantic attraction to a degree I had never experienced before. Because of our hierarchical professional relationship and my marriage, anything beyond a collegial friendship was out of the question.*

Maryam scheduled a life between lives session in hopes of understanding the lessons her soul incorporated into this lifetime and her inexplicable feelings for Daniel.

> *I am very interested in gaining a deeper soul perspective on my relationships to help me to move through the associated emotional difficulties. I want to know what I came here to learn in regard to these relationships.*

Maryam also hoped that she would find a way to cope with what, over the course of several years, had become an unbearable longing to be more than Daniel's friend. She also hoped to discover the soul agreement she made with her husband and her spiritual connection with her friend, Justine.

In a first past life regression, Maryam identifies herself as a young slave girl who is overcome with grief. She has lost her beloved Rau, who was beaten to death in her presence. She is locked in the horror of seeing him cruelly treated as he attempted to protect her from the master's mistreatment. She is carrying guilt for being unable to intervene. In response, she has run away without a plan for her own survival. Understandably, she is terrified.

As is sometimes the case when a person is prompted to move to a different point in the life that they are reviewing, Maryam finds herself in yet another lifetime. She is now an older woman sitting in front of a fireplace in a cozy bungalow. It is the early 1900s. She lives a simple life, living by herself with her dog. She is happy and content. Others consider her eccentric, which pleases her. She knows that she has one treasured possession, a gift from a dear friend who Maryam recognizes as her close friend Justine in her current lifetime. She has a vague sense that she may have had a female lover who has already died.

Once again, while intending to move ahead to the next most significant scene, Maryam again goes to a different lifetime. This time she is an older man who has just died of natural causes in the presence of his wife and three adult children. A fourth child died many years before. He was a farmer who had a hard but satisfying life. He is known as a reliable and loving family man. Maryam recognizes the man's wife as her close friend Justine, and one of his children as her current husband.

From this higher vantage point in soul state, she can look back through the various lives just revisited to uncover the common theme and to glean the wisdom that each has to offer. It is that *love only appears to disappear.*

> *Once the experience of love seems lost, we must go within to find strength and courage. We must trust ourselves. Love is never gone. Love is deeper and stronger than the human experience of it. It is eternal.*

Maryam returned a month later for her life between lives session, having prepared an autobiography and her list of questions and issues that she was seeking insight about. The process of writing the autobiography is a means of honoring yourself for what has brought you to this point in your spiritual development and exploration. The list of questions provides the focus for the session.

Maryam moved into a deep state of trance quickly, as a result of her experience in the first session. She vividly recalled her time in her mother's womb. Her higher self joined the fetus during its sixth month and immediately felt her parents' intense love and their excitement about her upcoming birth.

Maryam shares that her plan for the upcoming lifetime will challenge her to know who she is at her core. The plan also includes building emotional strength and confidence, overcoming fear, and bolstering personal power. To facilitate this, she has selected a body whose nature is timid and sensitive. The role of *good girl* will launch her toward goal achievement.

Like many other souls, the path to accomplishing life goals will unfold through contrast and opposites.

Before heading to the afterlife, Maryam moves into a past life. Once again, she is revisiting the lifetime of the young slave girl who has run away. She is being hunted by a group of men. She is not able to outrun the dogs that they have brought to track her scent. They find her hiding under a hollowed-out tree and drag her through the forest. She is resigned to her fate.

> *I just gave up. I didn't care. They killed me.*

Floating out of her body, she says that her plan had been to develop strength and courage in that life.

> *Both propelled me to run away and to try to free myself. My life didn't matter without freedom. I demonstrated that I had strength and courage even in this short life. I didn't let them beat me down.*

Before moving on, she connects to the mother of the slave girl. She instantly understands the deep connection she felt to her mother in the womb. In her life as Maryam and the life of the young slave girl, the same soul assumed the role as her mother. Her connection is very emotional, bringing Maryam to tears.

Maryam experiences movement through a vast field of countless lights, each light the manifestation of a different soul. Upon arrival in the interlife, she is greeted by Thesius, one of her guides. Thesius greets her by her eternal name—Serin.

Serin floats peacefully through a wonderous garden of healing.

Thesius tells us that the slave girl and her lover Rau were one and the same soul that split its energy in half to concurrently experience love from this dual perspective. It is the same for Maryam and Daniel, although their soul plan did not assure that they would experience love as a couple.

Thesius elaborates.

This has not been a common choice for incarnating souls, although now more are planning such an experience. It is quite challenging for humans.

Maryam and Daniel are one and the same soul. They are of the same energy. This decision is related to how love is experienced differently on the earth plane and on the spiritual plane. On earth, love is experienced in relationship with others. On the spiritual plane, love is the oneness.

The choice Serin made enables one to bring more divine love to earth. Serin decided to experience both simultaneously to integrate the two experiences of love.

Humans experience love as a positive feeling and as attachment to the subject of those feelings. Accomplishing the integration that Serin planned will require moving beyond attachment. It is not by being united with Daniel, although that might become a part of their future experience. It is found in the wholeness and completeness found within one's self. It first must be found within before it can be shared. Everything is within.

This path to self-love is among the most challenging, it is akin to a triathlon for the soul.

The sadness that people experience when love is lost or not reciprocated is the soul's yearning for completion within itself. It is a part of deepening its capacity for love.

Since it individuated to have separate experiences in human incarnation, the soul has longed to fill the void created through its separation. Similarly, it has yearned for remembrance of its divine essence and the experience of absolute love. After the long and unsuccessful search to find it in myriad lifetimes, the soul realizes that it can only be found within.

The scene shifts, and Serin finds herself surrounded by a brilliant light. She identifies it as the light of Source. She is filled with its loving presence. She lingers in the bliss.

In time, Thesius escorts Serin to meet with her council of senior advisors. They are gathered in a vast space. She sees a group of seven light beings. One of them begins.

Serin chose a challenging path. She planned to develop self-reliance and self-confidence, unconditional love, and love of self. She wants to develop trust in her higher self. She is doing well, despite the challenge and complexity.

She is learning to look within for her answers. In doing so, she is becoming aware of her strength and power.

The challenge is within, less with external circumstances. She is moving away from depending on others to depending on herself. Initially, she looked for answers outside of herself. When the people in her life didn't deliver, she turned inward.

She planned to heal the insecurity and self-doubt that have fed her need to depend on others. Her relationship with her husband showed her one way of not being attached and not needing others. Although it isn't her way, it prompts her to find her own way. She showed him that he didn't have to be so completely detached from everyone. These are the lessons that they incorporated into their soul agreement.

Her relationship with Daniel is a hurdle, it's her Mt. Everest. It requires patience, perseverance, internal strength, and not giving-up, especially when she doesn't have the emotional strength to keep going. It pushes her past her spiritual limitations.

Serin is in the process of fully awakening to her divine essence. Ultimately, she will discover that all along—she has been one with Source.

This is Serin's goal, but there were some remaining obstacles. So, she chose to split her own soul energy into two. Turning inward is accelerating her spiritual growth and clearing the path for her to come back to oneness. It is pushing her past what she thought she could do.

Specifically, Serin's relationship with Daniel provides a way to develop greater openness and authenticity, strength, and courage. It is not yet time for Daniel to know about the role he is playing in Serin's soul plan. This forces Maryam to work harder to achieve the objectives set in place in the plan. She is handling it by herself for long-term gain. Serin set it up this way. She knew that otherwise, Maryam would have looked to Daniel for answers. This will expedite her spiritual growth.

Serin is being given the assistance she needs. Her friend Justine is an example. They have been together through many, many lifetimes. She and Serin are soul intimates who enjoy a deep loving bond. Their synchronistic relationship provides each mutual support.

As the session drew to a close, the council members offered these closing thoughts.

> *We are not just going to hand answers to her magically. But assistance is there each time when Serin needs it. She must continue the work. She needs to keep going, she is close to getting there.*
>
> *Serin is stronger than she realizes. She is like the caterpillar who is in the process of emerging from the cocoon. She is whole in herself, as well as a part of the All.*

Once out of trance, Maryam described that a dramatic energetic shift had taken place. Most notably, her sense of *desperation* regarding her relationship with Daniel had *evaporated.*

The insights she gleaned from her sessions freed her to concentrate on the spiritual goal she set for herself. Her follow-up note says it best.

> *I sought out past life and life between lives regression in the hopes that it would help me to deal more effectively with a complex and emotionally difficult life situation. While I had obtained a considerable amount of spiritual assistance already, and had cultivated a regular meditation practice, I continued to struggle with a level of emotional despair that was intense and pervasive, seemed out-of-proportion to the situation, and at times impaired my day-to-day functioning.*
>
> *In both the past life and life between lives sessions, I discovered information that helped to explain the reasons for the intensity of my emotions, and the growth my soul was seeking to obtain.*
>
> *But the transformation I experienced cannot be explained by this information alone. Something about the experience itself created an energetic or spiritual shifting. There was a lifting of the emotional heaviness; a greater perception of connection to Source; a deeper awareness of who I am. I am experiencing greater equanimity, and I feel more empowered and capable of taking on the path that my soul has chosen.*

The clarity the council provided about the process and lessons contained in Serin's plan have applicability for all.

Once birthed as separate souls, each person reincarnates through a long series of lifetimes. In most of these lives, you are embedded in families and communities and experience much of life in relationship with others. These relationships help you to grow and expand your emotional capacity.

Over the course of many lifetimes, you become consciously aware that something is missing, and your soul yearns to fill the void. You try to fill it through loving relationships with others; relationships that are expressions of divine connection. Some of these relationships are satisfying, others are not.

As you grow spiritually, you awaken to the idea that what you had searched for externally could be found within. Over time, your sense of this grows, and you begin to prioritize deepening your capacity to love yourself. In doing so, you are beginning to awaken to your divine essence.

* * *

In this next case, we meet Luciana. As you will see, she is well along the spiritual path and has begun to enjoy the benefits of awakening.

LUCIANA

Luciana is a 54-year-old physician whose holistic practice is geared toward the integration of body, mind, and spirit. She is happily married and has two beautiful and gifted teens. Her current family life is markedly different from her own childhood. Her mother abandoned her, and she was raised by her grandmother and an unmarried aunt. Her memories of her father are dominated by his molestation of her on a visit to her parents, who resided in another country.

She coped with the emotional trauma of her childhood and youth by excelling in school, a choice that directed the course of her adult life, including graduation from a prestigious medical school. Despite outer indicators of success, she never felt as if she fit in. When her first romance ended, she experienced it as yet another abandonment.

Luciana realized during her medical internship that she excelled at *diagnosing and feeling other people's disease and pain.* As this acuity increased, she became fearful and prayed for it to be *shut down.*

She is an active meditator and found, as her practice deepened, that the visions that she blocked decades ago returned. She considers herself spiritual and hoped to explore her spiritual lineage during her life between lives regression.

Once in trance, Luciana finds herself in the life of a man named Mauricio living on a Greek island. He is married and has two children. He is employed as a writer for a journal focused on societal issues. He is passionate about ideas and is involved in promoting the well-being of his fellow villagers.

Mauricio moves ahead in life and finds himself on his last day. He is 84 and has enjoyed a long and happy life. He shares that he had a strong sense of belonging with the people and enjoyed a rich family life.

> *I have sadness leaving all of them but a sense of completion for having lived a fruitful life—through my heart. I feel that my heart is so big.*

Mauricio shares his reflection on his life in hopes that Luciana will carry this wisdom forward in her heart.

> *Love is everything. Appreciate the simplicity of life, love your family, love your neighbor.*

Luciana returns for her LBL session two months later and descends into a deep trance. From her mother's womb, she easily shares her early experiences, including the merger of her soul self with her mother during the fifth month of pregnancy. The physical limitation of the womb prompted her to use the time before her birth to allow her consciousness to reconnect with the souls in her soul family.

> *I am ready to leave the womb. I have been out and about, spending time with my soul family.*

She connects to the energy of her soul friends.

They are like small angels; they are sparkling and playful. There are so many of them. They want me to know that I will have company on my journey into this upcoming life. They want me to know that I will not be alone. They are so rambunctious; they are going to have to quiet down. They are reminding me not to lose sight of the levity that can be found in life.

Luciana understands that her upcoming life is intended to give her more opportunity to develop *independence.*

This is not so easy, because I am docile and dependent on others. I am excited about the life ahead.

Luciana moves quickly through a past life. She is a woman in her twenties, enjoying life in the English countryside. She writes poetry. She is visiting her dying grandmother who has had a long and happy life inspired by her faith.

She is not sad, nor am I. It seems others don't understand, but I understand why she is happy.

She moves ahead to the last day of her own life. She is 62 and surrounded by her children and has been ill for some time. As she floats out of her body, she shares.

I understand something about death that my grandmother shared with me. It's like changing clothes.

My form is changing, it's disappearing. I have become a being of light. It's so airy. As I go fast, I lose my density. I barely recognize my form, but I know who I am. I see the lights of twinkling angels. Everything is so ethereal.

I am being shown the way by a very strong energetic being. I recognize her as my guide. She is very strict. Her name is Pem. She radiates a blue light, and it is like a magic wand.

I have reached the interlife.

She is enveloping me in a cocoon of light, harmonizing and calibrating my energy. She's scanning and repairing my energy. I can feel light going up and down my being.

I am becoming bluer. The blue is becoming stronger. I have two stripes of blue.

She is telling me that I am more advanced than I think. Even though I have two stripes, I have been working with less than one blue stripe so as to fit into the earth energy.

Luciana learns that she brought 35% of her energy into her current incarnation. She bilocated, splitting her energy and sending it into a concurrent incarnation. This is not the first lifetime she has done so.

I am also living as a peasant in Tibet who is deeply connected with spirit. I did this to sustain quietness, a still point in my life. Part of me has to be very rooted in meditation. The other part of me is active so that I can function with the collective.

Luciana's higher self explains that she is part of a collective that is *connected to a different realm. The collective cultivates silence and quietude in the Earth energy.* In this current incarnation, her Tibetan-self is the direct link to the collective. Luciana elaborates about her incarnations, 27 in all, most of which have been in other worlds.

I am from a different realm. It is mostly an energetic realm, but there we can direct energy to manifest at will, including in physicality. In other dimensions, souls do not follow the same evolutionary path. Life manifests without biological evolution, without physical procreation by a mother and father. Some souls are already mature with no need to be raised by a mother. These souls do not need to go through a mother or father to experience.

The energy from my realm is different than earth's. The vibration of the energy is higher. I can't bring all of my energy into an earthly incarnation. I only bring part of it. It would be too much, and it would not prove useful.

I was sent to earth to help the transition of the planet. My purpose is to serve, to help humanity leap to high levels. I have been here several prior times, during times of transitions, two thousand years ago and four thousand years ago.

Questions arise about Luciana's current life, given the context and purpose of her incarnation. We learn from Pem that Luciana didn't need a mother in the same way humans imagine. However, she did have to rebalance the beliefs and feelings around abandonment that were residue from an earlier earthly incarnation.

Once in human form, she had the experience of needing a mother. Her mother's abandonment caused her much pain. But it also provided an opportunity for her soul to bring balance to her beliefs and feelings, thus furthering her spiritual growth.

Pem elaborates.

> *Once you incarnate on earth, there are things that likely have to be cleared up, to be healed and balanced. This was the case for Luciana. Her experience with her parents set the stage for this to happen.*
>
> *Whatever is created on earth must be balanced on earth.*
>
> *In one earlier earth life, Luciana was being persecuted for her religious conviction. To save her daughter's life, she gave her daughter to someone else. Although she escaped death, she mourned the loss of the daughter she abandoned for the remainder of her life. This emotion needed to be balanced. In that life, she died at peace, sustained by her faith.*

As the session progresses, we learn from Pem that Luciana's higher self chose her career path because healing is transformative. The energy of those she treats is transformed through her care. She agitates old energy to move out and bring in new energy. It makes use of her *spiritual charisma.*

Luciana hoped that her LBL would provide her direction for how to heal the negative emotions that she carries for her childhood experience. Pem would not disappoint.

> *Luciana must go deeper and tap into her essence. She can then use that energy to feel more fulfilled. When you enter the earth energy, you risk getting trapped into the lower vibration. If she taps further into her essence, she will actualize more energy from her soul, and she will experience more fulfillment. Her soul expects this of her. It was part of her agreement to bring more light into the earth plane.*

Pem elaborates on the universality of Luciana's experience to all humans.

You must remain vigilant in order to perceive feedback from your soul. When you incarnate on earth, the density of the energy can trap you. You lose sight of your essence because you get trapped within your sensory experience. It is not so easy to allow your essence to unfold.

The essence of the soul is love and light. The journey of the soul is to know itself as love and light.

Pem has gifted all who seek spiritual growth with a clear reminder that when you incarnate on earth *with blinders on,* you are seeking to remember your essence as the love and light of the Creator Source. It is a message which resonates with those who intuitively sense that they walk the spiritual path.

In a follow-up session, Luciana expressed tremendous gratitude to Pem for the insight and wisdom she provided. In the months following her LBL, Luciana found that she was calmer, more confident, and happier. She shared that her patients have reported that their healing sessions have had more profound impact. She also discovered that a path had opened to forgive her mother. In deepening her capacity for love, she was able to do so.

Most profoundly, connecting to her eternal self and being reminded of her spiritual path has given her a sense of inner peace. After all, as Pem reminded her, her essence is the love and light of Source.

Mankind is engaged in an eternal quest for that 'something else' he hopes will bring him happiness, complete and unending. For those individual souls who have sought and found God, the search is over: He is that Something Else.

—PARAMAHANSA YOGANANDA

10

Divine Essence

Awakening to Love

You are eternal, individuated at an unknown moment in time to experience human life from a single vantage point. Long forgotten, you were crafted from the same substance as the Creator Source who brought you to life. From that moment eons ago, you have circulated through countless lifetimes in both physical and astral realms.

Teilhard de Chardin reminds us that *we are not human beings having a spiritual experience. We are spiritual beings having a human experience.* This is not merely a flip of phrase. It is a profound acknowledgement that the very core of our existence is first and foremost spiritual, and that human life is a vehicle for spiritual growth.

Your soul's mission through its myriad incarnations is to awaken to your divine essence. This is the driving force behind your many forays into earthly life. Each incarnation affords many opportunities to accomplish this. The limitless nature of eternity affords endless chances for growth—to learn, to heal, to balance, to serve, and through these, ultimately—to awaken to your divine essence.

In the realm of free will, there is no one way or timeline for this awakening. Each is free to choose the path and the timing. Once the soul has accomplished its mission, it is able to move beyond the interlife, what the Hindu saint Sri Yukteswar labeled the *ordinary astral Universe,* and enter the higher heavenly realms.

What we've come to understand about the soul is that this journey is anything but haphazard. The stories shared here have illustrated time and again how the soul readies itself for an upcoming lifetime by developing a plan for the life ahead. You have seen that these plans were deliberative and purposeful. Goals were incrementally achieved. Turmoil and upheaval were embraced as the pain of previous lifetimes faded.

We have seen through the shared stories how beliefs shape how you feel, and ultimately how you behave. Beliefs, feelings, or behaviors that are out of balance are impediments to awakening. As such, they provide rich opportunities for spiritual growth. Bringing resolution and balance to these can take many lifetimes. Paradoxical challenges are often the way.

Soul growth is driven by the need to master love and is expedited by deepening your capacity for love. This is facilitated and hindered by the fact that we spend most of our lives deeply embedded in relationships. Those we have met in prior chapters have shown us how the wisdom, healing, and balance sought is embedded in relationship challenges. Loved ones and others play major roles in the unfolding of soul plans, including when they have agreed to be cast as villains.

Through its victories and setbacks over time, the soul begins to develop love and compassion for others. Often after struggling for many lifetimes, it develops love and compassion for itself. In the process, it is deepening its capacity for love.

As the soul's capacity for love grows, it remembers its divine essence, forgotten and obscured so long ago. As it masters love, it opens the way for a full awakening to its divinity. Doing so opens the arms of God for a full embrace in the love, joy, and bliss that has awaited your remembrance.

What does it take to realize that you are divine and deserve self-love and compassion? For many, the first impulse was prompted by despair.

It was triggered by the anguish caused by the loss of a loved one through death, separation, estrangement, or abandonment. It was brought about by the lack of forgiveness of self or others for acts or inactions. It was caused by an inability to overcome doubt or accept oneself. It was an outgrowth of a low self-esteem. Or it was a natural by-product of an inability to prioritize and care for self.

Finally, it is the culmination of consciously accepting that you are a spiritual being having a human experience that ultimately leads you onto your spiritual path.

Growth has been achieved by those you have met in the previous chapters. They have accomplished this by beginning to overcome the challenges that have caused them great pain. Motivated by suffering and a desire to be free of life challenges, they journeyed through timelessness for understanding and healing. In the process, they have gained insights and wisdom. They uncovered the ideas, feelings, and behaviors that needed to be brought into balance.

It would be wrong to claim instantaneous success. No multi-hour session, series of sessions, or magic solution mitigates past suffering. Yet, for all of them, their pain has eased, their journey forward has been clarified, and their mission to awaken their divine essence has been affirmed. Each of them benefited from the wisdom and encouragement so generously shared from the higher realms. Each of them is more motivated, knowing that they are destined for success.

Awakening to your divinity is guaranteed to all, regardless of whether you are in a hurry or whether you are taking your time, enjoying the many distractions of earthly life. Regardless of the pace, you are in the process of heading back to re-emergence with the Creator Source.

As you move further along your spiritual path, you begin to have glimmers of the bliss that awaits full realization. Even once this milestone has been reached, you may not yet have learned, healed, or balanced all that you embedded in your soul's plan for this lifetime. The final push for this full realization includes tying up loose ends. But by this point in your eternal journey, as you get closer to Home, you begin to reap the rewards of your long voyage back. You are awakening to love, your soul's destiny.

Whispers from Eternity*

Among the hundreds I have regressed in my practice have been a handful of very advanced souls. It was an honor to engage with their higher selves and the higher beings who counsel and guide them.

Interestingly, none of them hinted or declared that this was their final incarnation. Like others, who might wish that this is their final lifetime, each of them was focused on engaging fully in life and ensuring that they were fulfilling their soul's purpose.

What does distinguish them from others is the importance of their spiritual life and practice, which in each case is reflected in the peace and joy that they radiate. It is their spiritual practice that is their ballast. Through meditation and prayer, they are deepening their connection to the Divine, which remains strong even during moments of tumult.

* * *

In the selections that follow, you will hear the higher beings who have whispered from eternity to coax them on as they make the final push to the ineffable joy that awaits us all.

Advik

Advik is 73 years old. A year ago, his wife of 50 years died. Raised without religion, when he turned 50, he joined a temple. Several years later, he began to take his meditation practice more seriously. As a result, over time, he has reached deep states of bliss and peace.

He scheduled a session to explore what additional spiritual lessons he has yet to learn.

---

* *Whispers from Eternity* is the title of a book by Paramahansa Yogananda

Once in trance, he finds himself in a nondescript space. He perceives diffused light centered in the space that disappears quickly, along with figures that were moving about. His attention is then drawn to a source of crystal-clear light which moves to the top of his head. Bathed in the light, he shares that this is akin to his experience in deep meditation.

The scene shifts, and Advik finds himself in a beautiful garden and settles onto a bench.

I am a body of crystal-clear light. It has an amorphous form that is similar to my earthly body. White light is emanating outward from my body.

I am no longer in the garden. I am in another world. It feels familiar, I have been here before. I come to visit sometimes. Now, the scene is changing again. It's very soothing. I am rising-up toward a light that is above me.

I feel like pure soul, going toward the Creator—the ultimate Divine. The light is becoming bigger and brighter. There is not one source-point of light, it is everywhere.

The light wants me to know that I am ready to merge with it, but there is some unfinished business that I must attend to. I am supposed to help mankind. I am being told that my presence is needed in the world. As my energy radiates out, it is helping balance other energies on earth. I am serving as an energetic anchor point.

I am told that there is nothing else I need to do. Just be.

The energy that is radiating out is intelligent enough to know where it needs to go.

I have the sense that other beings have joined me. They have come to give me blessings.

They are done now, some of them have disappeared.

There is a shift in the session, and information about a prior life flows.

I have had several hundred lifetimes on earth. I have incarnated elsewhere, but earth is my favorite. I love the atmosphere here. One of my favorite lifetimes was in India in the 1700s. I lived in an ashram and spent my time meditating.

The shift created an opportunity to ask the singular question that Advik hoped he would get answered during the session. It pertained to what he considers his exaggerated emotional reaction to seeing animals lying dead in the road.

The question shifts his attention to a lifetime in Asia in 1430. He is a leader in the Kahn dynasty.

I am riding a white horse, leading a huge army of men on horseback. I am feared. I am protected by metallic plates hanging on the front and back of my torso. My head is also covered with metal.

We are the aggressors. Many people are dying. I have killed many people and animals in this and earlier lives as a warrior. There was a time that I enjoyed killing, but now I consider it my duty. It is a necessity. I don't have guilt, but I don't like being so feared.

I have no friends, but there is a woman waiting for me back home. It feels like we have been together for a long time, although it has not been too long because I am often on a military campaign. She doesn't fear me.

We move ahead to the last day of the warrior's life.

I have been wounded. I am surrounded by my troops. I know that I am dying. It is an honorable death. I am telling my men, I did my duty, do yours.

Advik describes seeing himself float up and out of his body.

I am riding on a beam of light, moving up. My fears have evaporated. I have finished an aspect of life and can turn my attention toward my spiritual growth.

I have no personal regrets. I do wish the wars might have ended sooner. It was my decision to continue conquering territory and people.

I can see from this perspective that it was not about conquering. It was about overcoming my aggressive inclinations. My aggressive tendencies needed to be dissipated. My soul intended for me to come to understand the futility of war. This is a lesson that I could not learn in the abstract. Each soul must learn and reconcile it through their experience and actions.

I now understand the futility of all of the warfare. That lesson enables me to help other people in the future.

In lives to come, I will need to balance this, including spending more time dedicated to spiritual growth. I incurred a karmic debt to the many people I killed. In the future, I will work to balance that by serving those souls.

Advik's session illustrates that human incarnations provide endless opportunities for serving others and for learning, healing, and balancing actions taken in prior lives. In his case, his soul plan includes service to humanity in a manner that allows him to balance the *karmic debt* he incurred in his warrior lifetimes.

His experience is a reminder to all of us that mastery of love of self and others may be slow and incremental, but our success is assured.

Even for an advanced soul, there remains work to do. For him, radiating his energy is helping to balance other energies on earth.

His journey into the astral realm has provided a taste of what awaits all, a return to the Creator Source. Nothing can equate with the rapture of embrace in the light and the love that is everywhere.

Each of us is on a parallel journey with many unknowns. Like Advik, our path may be windy and cycle through hundreds of lives. What is known is that having individuated into separate morsels of the Creator eons ago, we are destined to reemerge with the Source.

* * *

In the next instance, we meet Nancy, who, like Advik, is tying up loose ends, and while doing so, is deepening her capacity for love.

Nancy

Nancy is a 64-year-old acupuncturist. She is intuitively gifted and finds this enhances her diagnostic abilities. Despite its obvious benefit for her patients, she keeps this acuity hidden from her more traditional circle of friends and extended family.

Her transpersonal journey was an outgrowth of her interest in metaphysics and not scheduled to address any specific life issue.

Once in trance, she finds herself on a rocky surface on the periphery of a smoldering volcano. Her form is pure energy. She is at the gateway to another reality, at a moment within *no time.*

She is welcomed by an energy being that refers to itself as One and offers this introduction.

I am the awareness Nancy channels sometimes, but there are others.

I'm from everywhere. I have singularity, but am all one. I have come to earth at the beginning when the earth was in its early formation. I come here to relax and remember. It's comforting here. I have come to remember possibilities. There are all kinds of choices, infinite possibilities.

One elaborates on what is guiding the exploration today, and in general.

Today's experience for Nancy is about her remembering that she is part of the One, to feel the totality. Within creation, nothing is impossible. We need to remember who we are and where we come from. The experiences that people have on earth are illusions.

I have come today to tell her to just be.

Those on earth are in the process of shedding layers of outdated crust as part of the ascension process. Progress is being made on this aspect. As the process accelerates, it will be easier to live, ideas will flow more freely, boundaries will be broken, and healing will increase.

The ascension process is healing perceived separation. People will realize that they are not separate from the One. Beings choose to experience separateness. It is a choice which begins the journey back to oneness.

The One responds to a question about the seeming paradox of the journey outward into separateness, only to begin the journey back to oneness.

It's a manifestation of creation, to see where it leads, with the hope that it comes back.

Those who choose to incarnate on earth are choosing an adventure in this realm. To do so, they are steeped in the illusion of separateness. Through the choices of many to experience this adventure, the earth's ascension is facilitated.

It's kind of like bees in a hive. Everybody has their job because they are part of the hive.

Prayer, benevolence, laughter, and love move the ascension process along.

The mention of love redirects the One's teachings.

Love is energy. Love is glue. It is the space between everything. When we recognize that space, we experience the feeling of love. All you need is love.

Love is a source of creation.

The One offered a beautiful analogy to make sure that this point was understood. The image of Michelangelo's Creation of Adam that adorns the ceiling of the Sistine Chapel is brought to focus.

Look at the hand. It does everything physical. It is an instrument of physical creation. You move your hands in limitless fashions to do limitless things. It delivers. In the same way, you are instruments of creation.

Everything is in our hands. The Universe is in our hands, creation, love.

Nancy uses her hands in her work. They are the instruments of healing. The hand is the instrument of human touch. It connects you to the source of love, which is one of the reasons it is so essential.

Nancy's healing will be easier over time. She needs to help people to understand that struggles don't need to happen. People shouldn't trivialize their experiences, but at the same time, they should not struggle with them.

The One was emphatic that the best thing that earth's inhabitants can do is to remember that they have chosen to experience an earthly adventure. They have donned an illusion akin to a costume worn by a character in a play. It's also important to recall that as the writer, director, star, and casting director of that play, you have chosen the costume that best fits the script, theme, and moral of your play.

It may seem irreverent to share that when the session ended, Nancy and I laughed uncontrollably for minutes. Certainly not at the material that was shared, but at the challenge of conversing with the highest level of consciousness that had identified itself as the One. Even in her deep trance, Nancy could sense the communication gap that we were experiencing. Our human limitations don't automatically evaporate just because we are able to traverse higher dimensions.

As the person posing the questions, I was mindful throughout the session that the One found some of the questions I posed difficult to answer and others ridiculous. At many points, there were long periods of silence, which the One would later note was so an answer could be expressed in a way that might be understood by humans. Conversely, some of the One's answers were incomprehensible, even with lots of probing for clarification.

People experience their journeys through the astral realm in many different ways. Even when there is the familiarity of return, the difference between the realms does not dissipate. Awareness is split between here and there, two different worlds, two different realities. Most of those who make or facilitate these journeys agree that the insights, wisdom, and healing achieved make the challenge more than worthwhile.

* * *

Finally, we are introduced to Nadir. You will see from his experience the reward that awaits the full expression of our divine essence. For certain, the journey is long and arduous. But equally certain is the richness of sublime love, joy, and bliss that awaits.

NADIR

Nadir is a 55-year-old chemist who migrated to the United States following a war in his homeland. Currently engaged, he was married previously but has no children. He is passionate about science and poetry. He has an *inexplicable* facility for automatic writing.

He scheduled his session in hopes of deepening his understanding of the meaning of life and to allay some of his doubts.

Once hypnotized, he finds himself floating in the darkness.

I don't have a body. There are countless stars and some redness. I am beyond the earth and its Universe. I am in the emptiness. That's where everything is. I've been there before. It's familiar… It is home.

I'm relaxed. There are no worries here. Nothing to doubt or fret about! Everything is just so beautiful. I must remember that I can dissipate my doubt and worries by looking up at the stars. They are divine sparkles, and they pulsate within.

I have returned to be reminded that there is nothing to worry about. I have been longing to remember. Everything is perfect. It's always been like that.

After a few minutes luxuriating in the emptiness, Nadir is greeted by the Guardian of the Gate at one of the access points to the vastness of the higher realms.

She has come with a reminder for Nadir and all who journey to awaken to our divine essence.

You come down to earth in disguise. You are like secret agents. It's just fun sometimes, just to enjoy it. It's all been planned by the vastness.

But earthly life is just like being in a play in which you play a role. Just play the roles. Put yourself in the role and just enjoy. It's like crossing a river to experience the other side, and then you return.

Remember that it is just a journey.

Sometimes you forget the fun part as you experience the contrast between pain and love. You have to know the pain to experience the love. Contrast is your teacher. Sometimes you even begin to attach to the pain, accepting it. But you must remember that the experience of pain and heartache is just for experience.

The journey, including the illusion, is for the sake of love. It's all about love, it's never without love.

It is hard for some people to experience the love of the vastness. They turn away.

They see their shadow and they mistake it for the light. Imagine that you turn your back to the sun, and you think what you see is the light. When you turn around and look at the sun, the shadows disappear automatically. Everything is light.

On earth, you struggle. You choose to turn away from the light. It's neither good nor bad. It's a choice to be turned around, to have a different experience. You get scared when you see the shadow. Some of you start running in the other direction. All you have to do to end the struggle is stop and turn back. That's all you have to do.

There is no inherent darkness, there is always light present. Darkness is an illusion. Turning away from the light creates the perception of darkness. But just like seeing the sun, if you turn around you will see that the light was always there.

There are those who temporarily turn toward the darkness. You call them evil. That too is a choice. It's just the experience. They go on ignoring their essence until they are done with that experience and remember that they too are of the light.

It's just life, but the journey pleases you. There's no wrong and right.

The Guardian of the Gate reminds us about our connection to the oneness that is sometimes forgotten.

Humans have to feel separate to realize that they're not. They have never been separate. Each and every one is everything. The ocean is in the drop and the drop is in the ocean.

Even when the surface of the ocean is turbulent, it becomes very still as you go deep. Just dive deep below the turbulence of life. You will find that life is like the ocean. The turbulence was superficial, it's another illusion.

Everyone is always connected, even when they are not aware of the connection. No one is disconnected. There is always a connection, there was never no connection. Everyone is connected as one in this dance of life.

Those who feel disconnected just have to look at the stars to know that they are connected. We are all one. There was never a separation.

The Guardian of the Gate shifts focus to what lies beyond the gate.

The gate is an access point to higher realms. Nadir has gone through the gate to travel to the higher realms. He has learned to dive deep into the stillness. Those journeys have inspired the love captured in his poetry and his passion for science. Like the great ones before him, he is dedicated to the greater knowledge.

No one can go through the gate until they are ready. You have to be prepared. You have to be the same vibration to travel beyond the gate.

The Absolute is beyond the gate. It's beyond everything. Sometimes you sense its beauty. It radiates everywhere, the beauty radiates everywhere. It's all about love, it is all love.

It's the center of all centers. Everything revolves around it, like bubbles on top of the bubbles on top of the bubbles.

We are always moving toward the center. It is everywhere, and it is within each of us.

The Guardian of the Gate urged us to remember that we are on a journey, a journey to awaken soul.

The journey is all about love, unconditional love. Love has no opposite. Life has no opposite. Birth and death are opposites, but life has no opposite, there's only life and love.

You have to know the pain to experience the love, contrast is your teacher.

Love is the outflow of energy from the Absolute. The soul is a singular outflow of this universal love. And life is an experience of the outflow of universal love. All of it is the expression of the divine love of the Absolute.

Yours is the journey to awaken soul—the return voyage to the Absolute. It's a long journey, one you can delay but not abandon. We are all traveling at different speeds and traveling somewhat different paths. But what we share in common is the certainty that God, the deepest expression of love, awaits to welcome us back with open arms. This is the soul's destiny!

Message to Readers

I hope you enjoyed reading ***Awakened Soul*** and found inspiration to guide discovery of your soul's plan for this lifetime.

As you read throughout, understanding your soul's intention for this lifetime will help you to heal and balance unresolved matters, to deepen self-love and compassion and promote spiritual growth. If you would like to explore your soul's eternal journey on you own, I have created a hypnotically guided spiritual regression mp3, available for free download at www.JoanneSelinske.com.

If you believe the wisdom shared in ***Awakened Soul*** has value, I encourage you to share these ideas with your friends and family. To facilitate this, I have created an ***Awakened Soul Reading Group Guide***, available for free download at www.JoanneSelinske.com.

For those of you who love to read, libraries have been a rich resource. For others, they are a lifeline to the world. Their value promoting a thoughtful and knowledgeable citizenry can't be overstated. If you agree, I encourage you to ask your local library to carry this book. This small act will help the energy and insights contained in ***Awakened Soul*** to ripple out, touching lives and changing the world one mind at a time.

I welcome your thoughts about the book and hope that you stay in touch at www.JoanneSelinske.com.

Heartfelt wishes for the joy and peace that awaits the realization of your soul's plan for this lifetime. . .

Joanne

About the Author

Joanne Selinske PhD, Cht, is the author of ***Awakened Soul: Discoveries of Healing, Self-Love and Spiritual Growth***. She previously co-authored ***Wisdom of Souls*** *and* ***Llewellyn's Little Book of Life Between Lives*** for The Michael Newton Institute.

A mid-life career shift in 2006 afforded Joanne the opportunity to expand her interest in the spiritual forces that shape human decisions and behavior. After a three-decade long career as a social welfare executive and advocate for human rights and protections, she became a spiritual counselor and hypnotherapist. She is certified by the Weiss Institute in past life regression and The Michael Newton Institute in life between lives® hypnotherapy. Her spiritual regression and spiritual counseling practice are geared to promoting emotional and spiritual transformation.

Joanne teaches soul planning to audiences interested in understanding life purpose and uncovering patterns of beliefs, emotions and relationships.

Joanne holds advanced degrees in Marriage and Family Counseling/Family Studies, and Metaphysical Science and Ministry with a concentration in Transpersonal Counseling.

Joanne's spiritual practice and thirty years in social welfare reflect her belief that each person is endowed with an immortal soul which has the power to heal, liberate and transform the individual and the broader society. Her practice has touched hundreds of lives in addition to the thousands served through the social welfare programs and agencies that she led.

When she is not sharing discoveries about our eternal nature and journeys through her writing, teaching and speaking, she is devoted to her beloved husband, family and friends. She is passionate about gardening and travel and considers the latter one of life's greatest gifts and teacher.

Visit www.JoanneSelinske.com for more information.

Made in United States
North Haven, CT
08 December 2021